LIGHTING
THE WAY

LIGHTING THE WAY

Providing Compassionate Leadership in Sustainable Development

Robert Gilleskie P.E.

MILL CITY PRESS

Mill City Press
555 Winderley Pl, Suite 225
Maitland, FL 32751
407.339.4217
www.millcitypress.net

© 2024 by Robert Gilleskie, P.E.

All rights reserved solely by the author. The author guarantees all contents are original and do not infringe upon the legal rights of any other person or work. No part of this book may be reproduced in any form without the permission of the author.

Due to the changing nature of the Internet, if there are any web addresses, links, or URLs included in this manuscript, these may have been altered and may no longer be accessible. The views and opinions shared in this book belong solely to the author and do not necessarily reflect those of the publisher. The publisher therefore disclaims responsibility for the views or opinions expressed within the work.

Paperback ISBN-13: 979-8-86850-537-9
Ebook ISBN-13: 979-8-86850-538-6

For James, Henry, Eloise, and Will, hoping we'll show enough leadership to leave a better world to them and their grandchildren.

Contents

Introduction ix
1 Social Equity in Sustainable Development 1
2 Specific Need for Leadership in Social Equity 24
3 Leadership in Social Equity — Racism and Civil Rights .. 69
4 Leadership in Social Equity — Homelessness............ 93
5 Leadership in Social Equity—
  Food and Nutrition Insecurity 115
6 Poverty and Income Inequality 138
7 Social and Environmental Justice 167
8 Immigration, Refugees, and Asylum Seekers........... 195
9 Health and Health Care............................ 218
10 Summary and Conclusions 246

Introduction

Definition and Elements of Social Equity

This book is about social equity, or, in its simplest terms, the fairness of relationships between human beings. A more concise definition might state that "social equity ... refers to fair access to resources and opportunities and full participation in the social and cultural life of a community."[1] But it is also about leadership in social equity, or the behavior of managers, administrators, and even individuals in ensuring that the tenets of social equity prevail in all human relationships. While there are numerous tangible areas of social equity, many of which are included in the United Nations Sustainable Development Goals,[2] this book considers seven of the more common ones to demonstrate the application of leadership in their observance (or not). These are:

Racism	Poverty/Income inequality
Homelessness	Environmental/Social justice
Food Insecurity	Immigration
Health Care	

Examples of these failures in social equity are evident throughout the world. Even after the violent protests in the United States over civil rights in the 1950s and 1960s, there are still violations of basic civil rights, an example of which is the treatment of young African American men at a Starbucks in 2018.[3] There are thousands of persons without adequate shelter in the United States, including 134,000 homeless in California alone.[4] While many Americans strive to watch their weight and restrict calorie intake, there are also many who don't have enough to eat, and many even in this country and throughout the world who are starving. Poverty is rampant, not only in many parts of South America, Africa, and south Asia, but also throughout much of the United States, especially in the inner cities of large metropolitan areas. Income levels don't always reflect the value of work provided or differ vastly between the highest and lowest paid in society. Also, violations of social and environmental justice, in which certain minorities are effectively forced to live in blighted areas or are treated differently under the law, are common. For those living in the American southwest, the constant flow of migrants from Mexico is a constant reminder of the plight of refugees throughout the world for many reasons. Finally, while health care in the U.S. is more often debated as a political issue, many people in this country still go without even basic medical services, and health care as we in the U.S. know it is virtually non-existent in many parts of the world.

The types and degree of social inequity vary worldwide. In the U.S., the most common instances of social inequity are found primarily in the inner cities. For many reasons people of color have either gravitated to more crowded urban areas where housing is very limited or inadequate, and this has led to consequential problems of poverty, poor education, and even inadequate nutrition since large markets with a variety of healthy foods are not prone to locate in the inner cities. But even in more sparsely populated areas, issues of social inequity exist from the lack of good paying jobs, lesser availability of decent health care, and substandard public education.

Worldwide, such problems are even more pronounced for a variety of reasons. In Latin America corrupt government and violence have driven thousands of people northward to seek asylum in the U.S. In Africa and South Asia, a combination of incompetent or corrupt governments with undeveloped economies has led to extreme poverty, starvation, and rampant illness spread by contagious diseases such as the Ebola virus.

There are almost as many causes for these failures in social equity as the issues themselves. Probably foremost among these is the failure of governance. Jeffrey Sacks, the Columbia University economist, and consultant to the UN on sustainable development, goes so far as to say that good governance is necessary to achieve the economic, social, and environmental objectives of the UN's Sustainable Development Goals.[5] Whether it be plain incompetence, or, as is more often the case, corruption, the role of government in advancing social equity cannot be overstated. Government operations and policies determine more than any other factor the rise of social inequities among its citizens.

Especially in the U.S., a common cause of many social inequities is the negative perception of the differences in human beings according to race, religion, sexual identity, nationality, or other identifying feature. Case in point, beginning with the slave trade of the sixteenth and seventeenth centuries, African Americans were not even considered to be as human as Caucasians, and this perception advanced with the "three-fifths clause" of the constitution.[6] While this clause actually referred to the allocation of additional Congressional seats in a state according to a number determined by three-fifths of the African American slave population in that state, the clause is often mistakenly interpreted to imply that an African American is only three-fifths of a person. For this and other reasons, many people have historically considered African Americans to be less than totally human, which has led to varying degrees of racism. While the country has seen tremendous improvements in race relations, mistaken attitudes of fear and suspicion toward fellow citizens based on race still persist.

Similarly, many currently hold mistaken attitudes toward Muslims based on isolated acts of terrorism committed by a minority of the Islamic faith. Others refuse to accept the right of same sex individuals to marry and raise children based on long held beliefs about the fitness of such couples to do so.

Economics causes many social inequities, especially with regard to providing funding to address many societal problems such as hunger, homelessness, the absence of health care, and poverty. Government leaders too often come down on the side of reduced taxes rather than compassion for the needs of citizens. This concern for reduced government spending is often compounded with political concerns that it isn't government's role to provide a safety net for those in need.

In this regard, one of the most unfortunate causes of social inequities is blatant hatred for certain races, religions, and life style choices. The August 2017 demonstrations and counter demonstrations over race and ethnicity in Charlottesville, Virginia, displayed the worst in a culture that has still not come to grips with a history of racism, the many advances in civil rights notwithstanding.

But why should we be concerned that the many forms of social inequity even exist? The most basic reason is the bond we share with all human beings, and the implied obligation we have to treat each other with at least respect, if not kindness and generosity. Perhaps the best description of our obligation to one another is that of Pope Francis in his encyclical *Praise Be To You*.[7] While the main emphasis of this encyclical is care for our common heritage, the earth and its environment, an included message is concern for the poor, the homeless, the hungry, and disadvantaged others living on the fringes of humanity.

Another reason these issues of social inequity should be of concern to us is that they are often the precursor and indicative of other societal problems which can be mitigated by the actions of human beings in responsible positions (leaders). Among these are civil wars such as those currently in the Middle East, the causes of which are often poverty and hunger of the population, such as occurred in the "Arab Spring."[8] A population without job opportunities and the resultant poverty, hunger, and life sustaining opportunities eventually rises in revolt to demand these from its government. A better path for the leadership in these countries would be to do all in their power to provide these basic necessities of life.

Absent this leadership from existing governments, the climate is also ripe for terrorism by groups such as Islamic State in Iraq and Syria (ISIS), whose members cultivate population unrest to gain a foothold in these nations.[9] After that, it is a short step to the horrific acts of violence which these groups ultimately commit. For both the propensity of civil war in nations with populations desperate for basic life sustaining needs, and the rise of murderous terrorism, the U.S. Central Intelligence Agency (CIA) monitors closely the issues of social inequity in these nations.

But even in a more general sense, issues of social equity (or the absence thereof) deserve the attention of all human beings. All too common are the UN pictures of children with distended stomachs suffering from poverty and malnutrition in sub-Saharan Africa. And the crowded living conditions, lack of education, and absence of health care led to the devastating Ebola disease outbreak in Africa in 2014–2015.[10] Even in the U.S., with its more advanced state of health care, substandard living conditions and other issues of social inequity can affect the general population. In December of

2017 the City of San Diego experienced an outbreak of Hepatitis C which killed 20 people and infected 578, due to the unsanitary and crowded living conditions of the homeless.[11] Possibly more than any other failure in providing social equity to humanity, these outbreaks demonstrate the extent to which these issues affect us all.

Given the importance of social equity issues just described, it's important to consider ways to bring about changes in society by addressing their management. In other words, how do we get better in treating each other—especially those who don't have the wherewithal to improve their own lives? This, in turn, implies behavior change effected by those having an influence—or possibly achieving an influence—on homelessness, poverty, health care, civil rights, or any of the other issues of social equity mentioned earlier. This may be a government, institution, Non-Government Organization (NGO), such as the United Nations, or even individuals, who have the capacity to influence change. And this influence which can—must—influence change to avoid the negative consequences of social inequities described earlier is *leadership*. While there is no guarantee that even superb leadership at all levels of government and society will magically eliminate all instances of social inequity, it cannot be argued that the consequences of these continuing inequities are not serious enough that leadership must play a significant role in their management.

The first part of this book, covering chapters 1 and 2, provides, first, the context of social equity, as it's included in a definition of *sustainable development*, or development which considers the impact of present behavior on the development of future generations. In this sense, social equity is considered at least as equally important as activities affecting the environment and the economy of current generations.

This first part of this book also considers the role of leadership in managing issues of social equity as described above. But given the special relationship between leadership and managing these issues of social equity just described, the author presents seven leadership traits which are appropriate for managing social inequity.

The second part of the book consists of seven chapters each focused on an issue of social inequity described earlier. Each of these describes first, the current state of that inequity in society today. Then, the author shows how sustainable development is affected by that current state, and how leadership can provide the behavioral change necessary for improvement. Finally, the author provides examples of positive leadership in addressing issues of social equity in the world today.

References

1. Katherine Takai, *Pursuing Sustainability with Social Equity Goals*, November 10, 2014.
2. Jeffrey Sachs, *The Age of Sustainable Development*, pp. 462, ff., 2015. Columbia University Press, New York.
3. Chris Woodyard, *Starbucks' 911 call that led to Philadelphia arrests of two black men*, USA Today, April 17, 2018.
4. Liam Dillon, *Billions of dollars to help California's homeless population are piling up — and going unspent*, LA Times, March 25, 2018.
5. Sachs, *The Age of Sustainable Development*, p. 3.
6. Paul Finkelman, *Three-Fifths Clause: Why Its Taint Persists*, The Root, February 26, 2013.
7. Pope Francis, *Praise Be To You*, Ignatius Press, San Francisco, 2015.

8. *The Arab Spring: A Year of Revolution*, All Things Considered, NPR, December 17, 2011.
9. Joby Warrick, *BLACK FLAGS THE RISE OF ISIS*, Anchor Books, 2015.
10. *Ebola: Mapping the outbreak*, BBC NEWS, January 14, 2016.
11. Paul Sisson, *How did San Diego get its hepatitis outbreak under control?* San Diego Union Tribune, February 11, 2018.

1

Social Equity in Sustainable Development

I. Definitions and Background

In its most basic sense, social equity connotes the fairness of the relationships among human beings. For our purposes, it describes the interaction of human beings, and the extent to which they treat each other fairly, and how that affects the development of the human species. There are many ways to describe human development, or civilization, or the evolution of man, and they all involve social interaction, if, for no other reason, propagation of the species. But in the context of our discussion, social equity may be considered as a component of *sustainable development*, which may be defined as "development that meets the needs of the present without compromising the ability of future generations to meet their own needs."[1]

In this regard, social equity may be considered as one component of three necessary for true sustainable development, the others being the *environment* and *economics*. Taken together they are sometimes referred to as the *Three E's* and are often illustrated as *The Triple Bottom Line*, as shown in Figure 1-1.

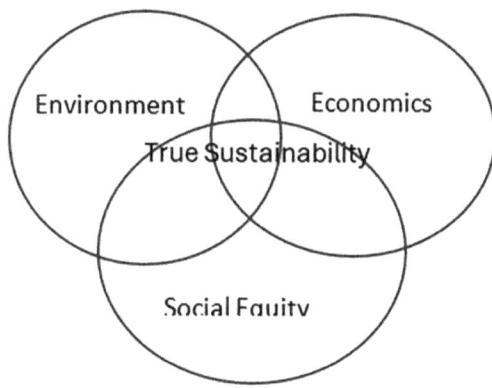

Figure 1-1. Schematic representation of The Triple Bottom Line.

Significantly, it is a fact that for "True Sustainability" to exist, all three components must be present. The Triple Bottom Line is sometimes also represented as the *Three P's*, in which the components are given as *Planet (Environment), Prosperity (Economics), and People (Social Equity)*. In either case each component implies distinguishing implications which are characteristic of sustainable development. Before looking more closely at social equity, it's appropriate to consider the implications of the environment and economics.

II. Implications of Environment

The environment is significant with regard to sustainable development in that it provides the support system for humanity and its growth—the earth, including its soil, oceans, rivers, and lakes, the atmosphere, including the very air we breathe, and all other living things including plants and animals. In spite of its massiveness, it's at the same time very fragile. Consider the proven hole in the ozone layer, which normally protects life on earth from the harmful effects of ultraviolet rays from the sun; the known hole in this protective layer has increased due to the release of chlorine-containing gases into the atmosphere. Or consider the life destroying sulfuric acid in the ponds and lakes of North America caused by the emission of sulfur dioxide from coal-fired power plants. Or consider the pollution in the Cuyahoga River in Ohio, in which the slag of pollutants became so concentrated that the river itself caught fire in the late '60s. Given just these few examples, it's only fitting that we explore ways to advance sustainable development by protecting the environment.

The ways in which we find, deliver, and use energy are among the areas most threatening to the environment if not managed responsibly. The dangers of acid rain from burning fossil fuels has already been mentioned, but other effects of using coal, oil, and natural gas to produce energy are just as harmful to the environment. Foremost among these is climate change, arguably one of the most serious threats to sustainable development today. Long a contentious issue, concern for climate change is growing more credible with more violent storms that have brought rainfall, rising sea levels, and protracted droughts throughout the world. It's becoming clearer that, for sustainable development, we, as a nation and as members of the international community), have to find better ways to find, deliver, and use energy.

Water use is another critical environmental concern. As with energy, the ways in which we find and use water have tremendous environmental implications. The Colorado River, which supports 5.5 million acres of farmland in seven western states, provides employment to 16 million people, generates $1.0 trillion in economic activity, and supplies potable water to 35 million people, and it is often virtually dry before it reaches the sea.[2] This is especially so in California, which receives essentially half its water from snow melt charging its reservoirs (the other half being from the Colorado River). This snow melt has been reduced due to the warmer winters brought on by climate change. In the Midwest, periodic droughts have forced an over-reliance on artificial irrigation and limited the recharging of reservoirs and aquifers. Such environmental impacts have spurred more sustainable approaches such as water conservation, recycling, and desalination.

Problems related to irresponsible waste management are the third major environmental challenge that is driven by human growth. Probably the most obvious result of this is the continuing buildup of the nation's landfills, which not only continues to exhaust given land area but possibly harms underground water supplies from the leakage of decaying matter over time. Furthermore, as the matter decays, it gives off methane, a greenhouse gas (GHG) with a global warming potential at least twenty times more powerful than carbon dioxide.

Another growing environmental concern, especially to marine life, is the amount of trash—especially plastic—that ends up in the ocean. While plastic bags from grocery stores are the most common culprit, there are numerous other sources of plastic that make their way into the ocean. Today, small beads of plastic are used in skin cleansing and makeup products, and after use, they find their way into the water treatment system, and eventually, the ocean. Marine life ingests these bits of plastic, and it accumulates in their digestive systems, which humans then consume as seafood. Fortunately, the public is becoming more and more aware of such plastic pollution, as an entire issue of *National Geographic* explores in detail the gravity of this environmental problem.[3]

Numerous other environmental issues exist which adversely affect sustainable development. Among these are the growing frequency of "dead zones," which have appeared in ocean waters offshore, usually at the mouths of rives. Typical of these is the one in the Gulf of Mexico at the mouth of the Mississippi River. Fertilizers and pesticides from farmland along the Mississippi River extending from the upper Midwest south to New Orleans are deposited by the river in the Gulf of Mexico where they provide nutrients for plant and algae growth. The plants and algae then use all the water dissolved oxygen, resulting in the dead zone. The process, termed *eutrophication*, is a continuing threat as farmers use more fertilizer to compensate for lost soil fertility.

Another environmental threat affecting sustainable development is the increase in forest fires caused, at least in part, by climate change. Increased temperatures and reduced rainfall lead to dried out forest growth, which provides ample fuel for more frequent and powerful fires.

III. Economics as Part of The Triple Bottom Line

In its most basic sense, *economics* is a social science concerned chiefly with description and analysis of the production, distribution, and consumption of goods and service.[4] But with regard to sustainable development, and especially The Triple Bottom Line, it is more correctly defined in terms of *economic growth* and, according to Jeffrey Sachs, economic growth measures the change in Gross Domestic Product (GDP) over a given period.[5] And these changes are a function of monetary flows throughout economies, whether they be international, national, or even state and local economies. Regarding sustainable development, pertinent issues are the costs of renewable energy, the dollar savings from energy conservation, or the costs of water reclamation or desalination, and many other quantifiable issues. All of these, and more, are usually considered under the blanket of financial economics.

But even more to the point at hand is the concept of *externalities*, as it pertains to economics and sustainable development. According to Margaret Robertson, "An externality is a cost that is external to the entity creating the damage."[6] Probably the most common example of a negative externality is the air and water pollution caused by an industrial facility, which benefits by not having to mitigate its emissions, but externalizes the costs to those affected by air and water pollution.

But there are positive externalities also. In compliance with the *Montreal Protocol*, signatories pledge to eliminate their production of chlorofluorocarbons (CFCs), which eat away the protective ozone layer above the earth. These CFCs are also very potent greenhouse gases (GHGs), which are one of the main causes of anthropogenic (manmade) climate change. By limiting the emission of CFCs, the Montreal Protocol also has the positive externality of limiting the production of GHGs.

In either case—negative or positive externality—the effect is to adjust the economics of The Triple Bottom Line—negatively in the case of negative externalities and positively in the case of positive externalities. As a result, Triple Bottom Line economics differs from financial economics in that the latter considers only well-defined monetary impacts whereas the former considers, and takes account of, less well-defined impacts. Admittedly, quantifying these externalities is usually very difficult, but they should always be recognized, and accounted for, at least in a qualitative fashion when considering economics as part of The Triple Bottom Line.

Another concept distinguishing Triple Bottom Line economics from purely financial economics is the concept of *natural capital*. Whereas human-produced capital includes resources such as machinery and money to make things, natural capital includes ecosystem services and physical natural resources.[7] While free to the earth's people, the benefits of watersheds and aquafers in purifying potable water surely have an economic value to all of humanity. Similarly, the Amazon rain forest benefits everyone by absorbing carbon dioxide (CO_2) from the air to limit the buildup of greenhouse gases and increased warming. While generally not quantified, such natural capital certainly provides economic value to the earth's inhabitants. In fact, a conservative value offered by most ecologists places the value of the earth's resources at about $33 trillion.[8]

One final differentiator of financial from Triple Bottom Line economics derives from the intergenerational aspect of sustainable development. Remembering that sustainable development is development that meets the needs of the present without compromising the ability of future generations to meet their own needs, it's important to consider the implications of our resource use today on the sustainability of these future generations. For example, what will be the final disposition of power plant nuclear waste with half-lives of thousands of years even 100 years from now? Or consider the effect of overfishing on the availability of seafood for future generations. While various studies exist, one predicts that available seafood will have declined by 90 percent by the year 2048.[9]

Also a result of the intergenerational aspect of Triple Bottom Line economics is the consideration of the future financial economic value of development activities undertaken in the present. Consider that $10,000 damage to the environment today, due, perhaps, to the loss of biodiversity of plant or animal species, would result in over a half million dollars of damage 100 years from now, using standard discounting and a 4 percent discount rate (1.04^{100} x 10,000 = 505,049). While somewhat contrived, this example shows the necessity of comparing present costs to the environment to those of the future.

IV. Implications for Social Equity in The Triple Bottom Line

The importance of social equity (or equality) has long been recognized both in the United States and internationally. Thomas Jefferson in 1776 set the tone for how the new government would treat its citizens in the Declaration of Independence.

> *We hold these truths to be self-evident, that all men are created equal, that they are endowed by their Creator with certain unalienable Rights, that among these are Life, Liberty and the pursuit of Happiness.*

And internationally, the Marquis de Lafayette, after the French Revolution in 1789, expressed the same sentiment with his words

> *Men are born free and equal in rights.*

In fact, since 1776 there have been about 120 similar statements throughout the world confirming the existence of human rights and the equality of all human beings.[10]

In 1954 racial segregation in public schools was ruled unconstitutional in the United States by the Supreme Court's decision in *Brown v. Board of Education*, but the issue remained unsettled for some time afterward. Separate drinking fountains for whites and "Coloreds" remained as a testament to racial tensions in Washington, D.C., into the 1960s. Riots in the Watts area of LA in 1965 showed just how bad the issues of race and prejudice by law enforcement had become. And this was again evident in the riots at the Democratic Convention in Chicago in 1968, and again in the race riots in Washington, D.C., later that year.

It was in this era of social unrest that a group of young public administrators met at Minnowbrook, New York, in 1968 and considered the importance of social equity in their profession. When one considers the work of Public Administration in its many applications—operating hospitals, running all levels of government, overseeing nonprofit organizations, managing educational institutions, to name just a few—it's no wonder that it (Public Administration) figures so prominently in defining and establishing the principles of social equity. In all these organizations the primary challenge is in leading and managing people (they are, in fact, two distinct things). In fact, it's not a stretch to state that the operations of all these organizations depend on how the people in them— leaders and followers—interact with each other. It nonetheless took until 2000 for the National Association of Public Administrators (NAPA) Social Equity Panel to define social equity as

> The fair, just and equitable management of all institutions serving the public directly or by contract, and the fair, just and equitable distribution of public services, and implementation of public policy, and the commitment to promote fairness, justice, and equity in the formation of public policy.[11]

The key words here are "fair, just, and equitable." While the words might seem to connote the same characteristic, there are some subtle, but important, differences among them. For one thing "fair" and "just" might seem synonymous, but "fair" connotes a legal aspect of treatment, whereas "just" tends more to a moral treatment or judgement. And "equitable" implies a comparison of the treatment or behavior of persons by others, as in treating different groups or persons the same way. As stated, this definition of social equity connotes not only the legal foundation for many social issues, but also the moral argument for treating others fairly. As a result, no segment of society should be treated with less deference than any other simply by virtue of their membership in that segment of society.

So important is this interaction among people to public administration that social *equity* has taken its place among the four pillars of public administration, the others being *economy, efficiency,* and *effectiveness*. In other words, social equity has as much to do with the successful functioning of society and the interactions of its members as these other more conventional elements.

And these interactions with people carry over into society in general, influencing the way we act toward, and refer to, each other. Evidence of this exists in the numerous social movements in modern day society. Consider the "Black Lives Matter" movement's reaction to perceived mistreatment by law enforcement of African Americans. Or the recent "Occupy" movement by young people protesting the economic and social injustice of corporate control over government and business in the United States. Or the international MeToo Movement in which women have come forth to protest sexual harassment in government, athletics, and entertainment. Such movements are indicative of a new awareness of the need for social equity in society.

Perhaps the most obvious illustration of social inequity in society today in America, but also throughout the world, is the polarization that exists among different groups of people. While this is most obvious between political parties in the United States, it also exists among those of different races, religions, and even ethnicities, and the effects of this polarization are especially harmful to sustainable development.

For one thing, government, especially the ability to legislate in Congress, is seriously damaged. Why else has Congress not been able to pass an immigration bill for decades? The most visible indication of this polarization was the violent insurrection at the Capitol on January 6, 2021. Related to this is the fact that hatred among different races, religions, and those with different sexual orientations is exacerbated more now than possibly ever.

Possibly one of the most convincing statements of the need of for social equity is contained in Pope Francis's 2015 encyclical *PRAISE BE TO YOU On Care for Our Common Home*. Especially regarding climate change, Pope Francis includes numerous references to man's obligation to care for the environment and his fellow man, especially the poor and otherwise disadvantaged. Typical of these messages in the encyclical is Francis' reminder that "a true ecological approach . . . must integrate questions of justice in debates on the environment."[12]

A. Why Social Equity?

The significance of social equity, both as part of The Triple Bottom Line, and its evidence (or lack thereof) in society, begs the question, why? One answer goes back to its role in public administration as described by Shafritz and Russel in their introductory text.[13] The first reason is the fact that its public administrators' duty to apply the law in a fair manner in dealing with all those for whom they are responsible. In other words, it's the law. Secondly, today's global, competitive economy requires more than ever a skilled workforce which cannot discriminate for reasons other than merit and education. Especially in the advanced sciences and technologies, the more capable persons may not be of one gender or even a native-born American, and a diversified work force often proves most competitive. Whether it be for Corporate Social Responsibility (CSR) requirements, or simply because one wants to do the right thing, observing social equity tenets in business and social life is the moral thing to do. This is especially true today, when young workers are looking for employment in companies that act responsibly in their relations with people.

A second set of reasons for which social equity is important considers its role in development. One consultant offers three reasons for which social equity should be a priority in the development of nations.[14] One, it's a given that there are certain factors people cannot control—race, gender, disability, to name a few—which should not preclude their sharing in the benefits of a society of which they are members. To do so, that is, to discriminate against them, could lessen their ability to contribute to the progress of that society. Secondly, it is a fact that there are certain needs everyone has, such as nutrition, health, clean water, and personal security, regardless of their uncontrollable differences. To ignore these needs would reduce the likelihood of successful development of the whole, since these less advantaged people are a part of the whole. Achievement and position in society should be a result only of fairly judged effort and capability, since these are largely controllable by the individual.

A recent article in *National Geographic* describes the global consequences of social inequity, the author giving three reasons for which humanity should be sensitive to inequality.[15] First, there is the issue of health. The outbreak of contagious diseases in sub-Saharan Africa over the last few years shows the impact they can have not only on adjoining nations, but across the world. International attention to preventive measures such as hygiene and better living conditions for all the world's people benefit not only them but all of humanity. Secondly, as already noted, many nations, especially in the Middle East, are ripe for terrorism, when people do not have access to secure, reliable sources of food and clean water. Again, action by international organizations such as the UN to provide for the world's poorest people can make them less susceptible to the influence of terrorists. Finally, there is the issue of "affluence envy." With the world's population currently at about seven billion, and approaching nine billion in the foreseeable future, it is inconceivable that everyone will be able to support the extravagant lifestyles of developed nations. As the people of Third World nations have more access to the internet and see these affluent life styles, they wonder why they can't live the same way. And it's a simple demographic fact that the earth's "carrying capacity" just cannot support it. A better approach might be to search for ways to reduce the inequality of people throughout the world.

B. How to Achieve Social Equity
1. Communities

So convincing should be the reasons for striving to achieve social equity, that the next logical question is how; that is, what should we be doing to achieve it? One recent study of how various communities approach social equity goals describes different strategies.[16] In all official documents and conversations by community leaders, members should try to explain social equity and its importance to the community. Examples of social inequities in the community such as poverty, social injustice, homelessness, racism, and inadequate health care can make clearer the dimensions of an otherwise abstract concept. For those communities developing sustainability plans, members should recognize social equity as an integral part. One way to do this is to put emphasis on The Triple Bottom Line, which considers social equity to be as important as the environment and economics. At the same time leadership in the community should coordinate with nonprofits such as the city's food bank and the Salvation Army to achieve common goals. Among these goals might be efforts to assist disadvantaged members of the community in satisfying basic needs. In all of these efforts, community leaders should use existing data to track progress in achieving social equity goals.

2. Nations

At the same time nations should implement programs to achieve social equity.[17] Almost all nations provide universal health care for their citizens, but those who don't should pass legislation to provide at least affordable health care. Not only does a healthier population enhance economic productivity, but reduced health care costs make nations more economically competitive.

Recognizing that every nation's population has disadvantaged segments, it is to national economic advantage to provide special care to those known communities. For example, many countries today provide inexpensive or free influenza inoculations to prevent the spread of that disease. The alternative is for people who can't afford the inoculations to go without and run the risk of spreading influenza. Similarly, nations should ensure a minimum level of wellbeing to all their citizens to preclude the effects of widespread poverty which affects the nation as a whole. We need only look to the success of the U.S. Social Security program to provide one example of how this may be done.

Insofar as a nation's political structure permits, it should distribute resources in an equitable manner. Recognizing that water in the earth is a resource belonging to all, steps should be taken to prevent its use by only favored segments of the population.

Nations should examine their existing power structures to ensure the benefits of government are available to all equally. In the United States, citizens should be aware of the inequity resulting from so-called gerrymandered congressional districts which provides unwarranted power to one political party over another.

3. Individuals

The opportunities for individuals to show leadership in social equity are many. Probably the most significant of these are the teachers and administrators in elementary and secondary schools, for it is here that attitudes of social interaction are formed, and next to family influence, children's concepts of others are formed at the earliest age. In this regard teachers and school administrators bear an especially pivotal responsibility in forming attitudes of social equity.

By the very nature of their calling, social workers also have daily opportunities to ensure social equity in society. In fact, it may be argued that the issues of poverty, homelessness, inadequate health care, income inequality, and social justice are nowhere as predominant as they are in the life of a social worker. As such, there is the continuing challenge—and opportunity—to support social equity in society. Similarly, welfare providers directly confront poverty in the poorest of the poor, and how well they do this is proportionate to the degree to which they are committed to social equity.

Unfortunately, vigilant law enforcement is necessary whenever people interact in society. But, at the same time, there are numerous opportunities for members of law enforcement to show practical support for social equity in their daily work lives. For example, in settling disputes between individuals, doing so in a completely unbiased way ensures fairness in the way justice is administered (social justice).

Those working in health service organizations have a unique responsibility in ensuring social equity. The very act of providing health care to those in need is an element of social equity, but doing so in a caring, thoughtful manner is even more so. Also, administrators in large health care organizations have a special responsibility to ensure fair treatment for everyone at fair and reasonable prices.

C. The Interaction of Social Equity with the Environment and Economics

An obvious question concerns the relationship of social equity with the other elements of The Triple Bottom Line—the environment and economics. As already illustrated, true sustainability cannot be attained without all three elements. But the question remains—how can these three elements bring together the essential ingredients of sustainability?

1. Social Equity and the Environment

One way to look at this is to consider each of the elements' effects on the other two. To start, one could look at the effects of social equity on the environment. For example, in general, lower income people have not purchased newer energy efficient vehicles, like hybrids and all-electric vehicles (EVs). As a result, there are still many older vehicles in use with their much less efficient technologies (fewer miles per gallon) and much higher emissions of Greenhouse Gases (GHGs). This, in turn, leads to greater pollution and diminished ability to fight climate change.

Another impact of social equity on the environment is the fact that poorer people cannot afford solar energy and many other energy saving devices for their homes. While the price of solar has come down drastically in the past decade, it is still out of reach for most lower income families. In addition, since many lower income families cannot afford their own homes, they are unable to install solar energy systems. While many Investor-Owned Utilities are now offering to assist in installing solar energy systems on multi-family residences, they are still primarily purchased by owners of detached homes, who are generally more well off. The inability of lower income families to install solar energy systems means that more electricity is produced by fossil-fueled power plants, emitting more GHGs.

One more impact of social equity on the environment is the proliferation of much higher density, neglected communities in which fewer services are provided and there are often higher rates of crime. Such environments generally have lower air and water quality (see Flint, Michigan) with adverse effects on adjoining communities

Just as social equity has adverse impacts on the environment, the environment often has adverse impacts on social equity. For example, blighted and polluted neighborhoods provide unhealthy living conditions for lower income people who cannot afford to live anywhere else. Similarly, lower-income people often must live near major transportation thoroughfares where air pollution is highest.

On a more global scale, rising sea levels often have a disproportionate effect on those forced to live near the coasts or on one of the many Pacific islands for reliable food sources such as fishing. The best example of this is the Marshall Islands, which stand to disappear due to rising seas caused by climate change.[18] A similar fate awaits the poor in Bangladesh, where it is anticipated that a

3-foot rise in sea level (projected for 2100) would displace 20 percent of its population.[19] What is particularly tragic in both these cases is the fact that the developed world, through its use of fossil fuels over the last 150 years, is the cause of climate change, but the underdeveloped nations will bear the brunt of its effects.

2. Social Equity and Economics

Probably one of the most glaring examples of the interaction between social equity issues and economics is health care. Consider first, the effect of social equity on economics. It's long been known that the per capita cost of health care in the U.S. is much higher than in other industrialized nations.[20] In fact, the United States spends almost twice as much per capita as other nations. While it may be argued that health care is so much better in the U.S. than other nations, this is generally not the case.

What is true is that the cost of manufacturing is higher in the U.S., partly due to this increased spending on health care. For example, it costs Daimler Chrysler AG about $1300 per car for health care for employees, whereas the health care costs for the same car manufactured in Canada is virtually zero.[21]

Another effect of social equity on economics is racial, gender, or sexual orientation discrimination in the U.S. work force. Oftentimes the best candidate for a position is a member of one of these minority groups, but that candidate is not selected because of his or her race, gender, or sexual orientation. In this day of global competition, such discriminatory practices cannot help but contribute to a competitive disadvantage.

Similarly, economics often has an adverse impact on social equity. Just as providing health care has an adverse impact on economics, the cost of health care unfortunately limits its availability to lower-income individuals. Steps to avoid this inequity, such as the Affordable Care Act (aka "Obama care"), and even suggestions for a universal health care system are attempts to prevent this social inequity.

Another example of the effect that economics has on social equity is the shortage of supermarkets and other sources of fresh food in lower-income neighborhoods. While so-called chain grocery stores stay away from such neighborhoods for various reasons, the lack of their availability nonetheless puts such communities and their residents at a distinct disadvantage. Community based food "Coops" and small "Mom and Pop" grocery stores provide some relief, but a larger Non-governmental Organizations (NGO) or local governmental effort is still needed to address this shortcoming.

The issue of homelessness is directly related to economics, that is, the ability of everyone to provide shelter for their families, to say nothing about home ownership, depends on their ability to pay the high costs of housing. To one extent or another, the issue of homelessness affects almost all urban areas of the U.S. Again, solutions to this issue will require governmental or NGO action.

V. Social Equity's Need for Leadership

A distinguishing characteristic of social equity issues is the fact that most, if not all, involve behavioral change. The seeds of racism require the modification of individual attitudes at an early age—usually by parents, teachers, and society. Social justice requires the willingness and courage to advocate for change, usually at the risk of unpopularity or even persecution. Humane treatment of migrants and refugees requires the willingness to step forward as agents of change. In all these cases, leaders must be willing and able to change behavior in society by their actions, which, fortunately, are subject to individual change.

Again, fortunately, there have been and there continue to be men and women who possess the leadership qualities to effect changes in social equity. Also, fortunately, in most cases, these leaders have made the conscious decision to develop in themselves the qualities that enable them to be agents of change. There is, indeed, benefit in looking at their lives to distinguish those qualities which were conducive in helping these men and women become agents of change in social equity.

VI. Summary and Conclusions

Perhaps the best way to characterize sustainable development, or development which meets the needs of the present without jeopardizing the ability of future generations to meet their own needs, is through The Triple Bottom Line, consisting of three elements—Environment, Economics, and Social Equity—all of which must be present for true sustainability.

The environment consists of all the resources in our natural world, and their implications on not only humanity, but on all living things. A convenient way to look at these resources and their implications is by considering the way we find, distribute, and use energy and fresh water, and how we manage the waste we create in these processes. Man-made climate change is possibly the most significant current impact of energy management, and sustainable development implies the need for energy efficiency and the use of renewable energy sources. Responsible water discovery and use is also a component of sustainable development, as is waste management to limit the amount of waste accumulating in landfills and eventually ending up in the oceans.

The economics leg of The Triple Bottom Line considers *the production, distribution, and consumption of goods and services,* but only insofar as it promotes sustainable development. And for this to occur, such growth precludes *negative externalities,* or harm that occurs to some from actions caused by another achieving benefits from the same actions.

Another distinguishing characteristic of Triple Bottom Line economics is recognition of *natural capital,* or ecosystem services and physical resources provided by the natural environment. Typical of these are clean water, wetlands, and the world's rain forests. Determination of the economic value of any human endeavor must include the value of natural capital for true sustainable development.

While usually listed as almost an afterthought of Triple Bottom Line components, *social equity* in many respects is the most important, for it addresses the timeless and internationally recognized rights of all human beings. Moreover, there are compelling reasons for all of humanity to recognize these rights, if for no other reason than the failure to do so has negative consequences for all. One example of this is the spread of contagious disease in underdeveloped nations if developed nations do not offer assistance and health care to people in need throughout the world.

Critical to interpretation of The Triple Bottom Line is the fact that each of the included elements affects, and is affected by, the others. For example, the effects of climate change and environmental degradation (environment) affect the most disadvantaged people (social equity) because they are forced to live in areas most affected by pollution, blight, and other substandard conditions. Similarly, externalities in the environment distort the economics of development, such as occur with air and water pollution.

Especially regarding social equity, leadership in government, business, and the individual, is critical for true sustainable development. This is so because issues of social equity are generally the result of the attitudes and behavior of human beings. As such, agents of change (leaders) in society can recognize and strive to mitigate the behavior of others to promote true sustainable development.

References

1. *Our Common Future*, (The Brundtland Report), 1987.
2. Maite Arce and Michael Conner, *Saving the Colorado River before the water runs dry*, THE HILL, February 2, 2017.
3. *PLANET OR PLASTIC?*, National Geographic, June, 2018
4. https://www.merriam-webster.com/dictionary/economic
5. Jeffrey Sachs, *The Age of Sustainable Development*, p. 16, 2015. Columbia University Press, New York.
6. Margaret Robertson, Sustainability Principles and Practice, p. 56, 2017, Routledge, New York.
7. Robertson, Sustainability Principles, p. 55.
8. Tony Juniper, *It's the economists, stupid*, The Guardian, June 4, 2008.
9. Charles Clover, *All seafood will run out in 2050, say scientists*, The Telegraph, Nov. 3, 2006.
10. https://www.monticello.org/declaration/
11. James H. Svara and James R. Brunet, *Social Equity is a Pillar of Public Administration*, ResearchGate, July, 2005.
12. Pope Francis, *PRAISE BE TO YOU On Care for Our Common Home*, 2015, Ignatius Press, San Francisco.
13. Shafritz, J.M. and Russell, E.W., *Introducing Public Administration*, Upper Saddle River, N.J.: Pearson Education, 2005.

14. Harry Jones, *Equity in development: Why it is important and how to achieve it*, Growth, Poverty & Inequality Programme, November 2009.
15. Jared Diamond, *The Global Peril of Inequality*, National Geographic, Vol. 234, No. 6, December, 2018.
16. Katherine Takai, *Pursuing Sustainability with Social Equity Goals*, International City/County Management Association, November 10, 2009.
17. Harry Jones, *Equity in development: Why it is important and how to achieve it.*
18. Michael Gresko, *ANTARTICA IS MELTING AT A DANGEROUS PACE—HERE'S WHY*, National Geographic, National Geographic, April 25, 2018.
19. Robert Glennon, *The Unfolding Tragedy of Climate Change in Bangladesh*, Scientific American, April 21, 2017.
20. *The Effect of Health Care Cost Growth on the U.S. Economy*, Final Report for Task Order # HP-06-12 Prepared for the Office of the Assistant Secretary for Planning and Evaluation, United States Department of Health and Human Services.
21. Downey, K. *A heftier dose to swallow: Rising cost of health care in U.S. gives other developed countries an edge in keeping jobs.* Washington Post, March 6, 2004.

2

Specific Need for Leadership in Social Equity

I. Leadership Background

Since social equity issues, such as poverty, racism, and environmental justice, involve the interaction and behavior of human beings, it only makes sense that this behavior can be changed. For example, attitudes toward, and treatment of, persons of color in society are a result of background and education, but these (attitudes) change over time, as evidenced by the treatment of African Americans since the 1950s. These changes did not just happen; rather, change primarily came about due to the influence of leaders in government and society, such as Frederick Douglas, Rosa Parks, and Martin Luther King. They, and many others like them, were agents of changes who provided the leadership to change the attitudes and behavior toward African Americans. They were, in a word, leaders.

The challenge these leaders faced was unique in that they were part of the marginalized segment of society for which they were fighting, but at the same time, they were also able to lead it. Obviously, as an African American, Martin Luther King was subject to the discrimination and injustice experienced by all African Americans at the time, but he was also able to influence public opinion and legislation. Among other positions, he was an ordained minister and president of the Southern Christian Leadership Conference. This relationship, in which the leader is both part of the marginalized group and at the same time in a responsible position with respect to it, has a significant effect on leadership. With respect to The Triple Bottom Line, an effective leader who is a member of a marginalized community can influence social equity issues much more than he or she can influence issues of the environment or economy. In this regard social equity leaders are probably more effective than leaders in almost any other human endeavor (military, education, business, government, to name a few).

Similarly, by the very nature of what they are trying to do (change perceptions and attitudes in society), social equity leaders face more resistance from those whose attitudes he or she is attempting to change. Consider those marching on "Bloody Sunday" in 1965 in Selma, Alabama, and the clubbing and other physical abuse the marchers endured to make their point. There is no other word to describe their mental set than courage. Such courage was proportional to the hatred they experienced from those whose views toward African Americans the marchers were attempting to change. There are few other instances of leadership in society in which courage has played such a dominant role.

One other characteristic of leadership in social equity is the extent of behavior, the "sea change" that such leadership brings about in society. It's almost inconceivable that before Susan B. Anthony, women were not permitted to vote in the United States. But with the leadership of Susan B. Anthony, women achieved the right to vote with the nineteenth amendment in 1920. Now they make up one of the most significant voting blocks in the country and have been able to change the culture and government of our country.

Or consider Mildred Jeter, an African American woman who married a white man, Richard Loving, in 1958 in the District of Columbia. When they later moved to Virginia, a state prohibiting marriage between two people of different races, the state prosecuted the couple and agreed to a suspended sentence only if the couple left the state. The couple later sued Virginia and the Supreme Court agreed with their suit, holding that Virginia's prohibition on marriage between two people of different races violated their rights under the fourteenth amendment of the constitution. Like the amendment granting women the right to vote, this decision changed the fabric of the nation due to the leadership of individuals believing in the justice of their causes.

One more example of leadership in social equity that resulted in long lasting changes to society is that of Harvey Milk. Milk was a gay man and stockbroker on Wall Street who moved to San Francisco in the 1970s to come out and operate a camera store while he was advocating for gay rights in that city. As his public involvement in the still growing gay rights movement continued, he eventually ran for office and became a City Supervisor in 1977. He was influential in passing a proposal to prohibit the firing of city employees for being gay. He was also instrumental in defeating California Proposition 6 in 1978, which would have prohibited gay persons from becoming teachers. But even in the more open-minded San Francisco, his civic activism in the gay movement was opposed by many, and another Supervisor, Dan White, assassinated Milk and Mayor George Moscone on November 27, 1978.[1]

It's almost inconceivable that popular sentiment—and the law—permitted such outright discrimination against gay persons as recently as forty years ago. This is especially true, given the number of gay office holders at all levels in the United States today. But Milk, through his leadership as an activist and Supervisor in San Francisco in the '70s, completely changed the behavior of society and the attitudes toward gay persons that had been prevalent at the time into what they are today.

II. A Characteristic of Leadership in Social Equity and Its Applicability

While it's difficult to specify exactly what type of leadership is best suited to issues of social equity, perhaps the ability of a leader to *empathize* with the feelings of others defines it best. It's important to emphasize that empathy does not imply a softness or unrealistic worldview on the part of the leader.[2] Rather, it does imply the ability of a leader to genuinely *feel* the unpleasant or even painful circumstances of another. Moreover, genuine empathy implies that the person having it works toward creating a better environment or improving the circumstances of the person or class of persons for whom the leader has empathy. In the examples of significant social leadership just given, the persons displaying leadership not only felt the plight of some marginalized individual, or even a persecuted class of people, but changed the course of history for that class.

Probably the most prominent application of leadership in social equity is in the field of public administration.[3] The role of public administration is a function of government at all levels—local, county, state, and federal—and as such, considerations of social equity are paramount in leadership. For one thing, it's the law. The Americans with Disabilities Act (ADA) requires government leaders to provide special accommodations and access opportunities to persons with disabilities. More generally, the Equal Employment Opportunities Act of 1972 prohibits discrimination based on race, color, religion, sex, or national origin. And there are many other such laws and regulations which ensure that leaders consider social equity in the performance of their duties.

But probably of greater significance is the fact that the way public administrators approach social equity provides a model for society in general. When governments consider race, gender, and sexual identity when they execute contracts, these same considerations affect the behavior and attitudes of those seeking to participate in these contracts. In general, members of society cannot help but modify their relations with each other based on what they see governments doing.

As a result, businesses, industries, and other institutions adapt their own attitudes and treatment of others based on what public administrators in government are doing. From the highest levels of management to all employees, people in most companies often find that treating others fairly is not only good for business, but it's the right thing to do. The leaders of nonprofits should be even more receptive to these principles, given the focus of what they are doing. Educators have a special role in promoting the observance of social equity. Many "sea changes" in social mores have started with children not seeing any differences in the races, religions, and genders of other children with whom they are playing. Their teachers have a special responsibility in describing to their students the social inequities of the past, such as racial segregation, and the evolution of human and civil rights legislation.

While social equity is not the first thing that comes to mind when discussing the military, it's worth noting that many social advances have occurred first in the armed services. Consider the fact that 180,000 African Americans served in the Union Army during the Civil War. Or that more than one million African Americans served their country during the Second World War. And in 1947

President Truman's Committee on Civil Rights formalized the government's attitude toward African Americans with the report "*To Secure These Rights.*" This report strongly condemned segregation based on race, color, creed or national origin" everywhere in the nation's military.[4]

Given the importance of social equity throughout government, business, and society, it only makes sense that there is strong leadership in each of these areas dedicated to the observance and advancement of social equity as an essential component of sustainability. While such leadership often reveals itself in many human endeavors, it is important that leadership dedicated to a commitment to social equity be given special emphasis. While many types of leadership can fulfill this need, leadership emphasizing sustainable development, especially The Triple Bottom Line, may best satisfy this need.

III. Leadership in Sustainable Development

The fact that leadership often falls short in fulfilling this need to advance sustainable development is evident from the absence of more compelling results. The most obvious example of this is possibly the refusal to accept anthropogenic (man-made) climate change, although almost three-fourths of Americans now believe it is real,[5] as well as 97 percent of published scientists.[6] And there are other issues of non-sustainable development for which no other reason for their lack of acceptance is evident except a failure of leadership.

An important element—if not the most important element—in bringing about lasting behavioral change, such as that in advancing sustainable development, especially in social equity, is getting people to want, deep down, to change their behavior. Dwight Eisenhower,

World War II General of the Army and thirty-fourth president of the United States, probably offered the best definition of leadership.

Leadership is the art of getting someone else to do something you want done because he wants to do it.

One type of leadership which specifically addresses the issue of *want* in is that described in LIGHTING THE WAY Providing Leadership in Sustainable Development.[7] This work approaches leadership specifically as it advances sustainable development, and more specifically, social equity as part of The Triple Bottom Line. In doing so, the work identifies seven traits which possibly best describe this type of leadership. These traits are *communication, vision, presentation, attitude, responsibility, respect,* and *empathy.*

Communication is simply how individuals in any undertaking convey information to one another by language. The two primary categories are written and oral, and each is critical in a leader's explaining to those led in such a way that they *want* the same thing that the leader wants.

Almost as critical as communication is *vision,* which is the desired result—usually long term—which the leader communicates to those led through written or oral communication, but the leader can deliver a vision simply by those activities he or she pursues in daily activities.

Sometimes called *charisma, presentation* is the sum total of communication and outward expression which creates a physical impression in those led such that they tend to approve of, and are more likely to accept, the message the leader delivers.

Attitude, usually qualified as positive attitude, is the outward impression, the message the leader conveys, that "Everything is going to turn out well." The leader may not necessarily have that internal feeling himself or herself, but he or she speaks, acts, and does those things which create the impression that the outcome will be good.

A familiar expression for *responsibility* is doing the right thing, especially when it isn't the easiest thing to know or do. An underlying assumption is that the person in a leadership position knows what the right thing is, and is willing to undertake it, regardless of the circumstances. Possession of the trait, does, of course, assume the integrity of the leader. In other words, the leader at least believes, in his conscience, that a given action is right, and is willing to pursue it even though the outcome may not be to his or her advantage.

Not as often heard among the characteristics of effective leadership is *respect*, which is simply recognizing that every person, regardless of their state or profession in life, has an inherent value which merits recognition simply because of their humanity.

Empathy is that characteristic in a leader which enables him or her to discern and actually experience the feelings, attitudes, and goals of those individuals he or she leads. By doing so, the leader can not only better understand what motivates the person led, but actually better align the things he or she wants done with the wants of the persons who are being led.

While each of these traits is characteristic of effective leadership in sustainable development, there are several which are especially appropriate to issues of social equity. Most issues of social equity throughout history have required arousal of the general populace—think civil rights, the MeToo movement, gay rights demonstrations, and other displays of public discontent—and it's obvious that effective *communications* have been an integral part of their success in each case. In all these it was necessary that someone or some group had to have the *vision* to translate a mere idea or passion into physical action on the part of ever larger groups of people.

The term *social equity* connotes doing the right thing, or responsibility. Often, pursuing the right course of action or having the right attitude, by most generally accepted standards, reflects one's decision to be responsible. Who can argue that racism is wrong, or that we have a responsibility to our fellow human beings simply because they are human? And yet, there have been times in the history of mankind in which this has been violated, such as the extermination of the Jewish people during World War II, the persecution of various religious sects, or even today, our collective refusal to ensure that everyone should have the basics of "life, liberty, and the pursuit of happiness." It's at times such as these when there is a need for leadership in social equity.

Related to this is the need for everyone, especially leaders, to have respect for their fellow human beings, simply because of their humanity. How many problems in society could we avoid simply by showing respect for others? And even more so is this true of our leaders in government and industry to show respect for those for whom they are responsible.

Possibly the most significant leadership trait in social equity is empathy. For if the leader can truly feel the deprivation, pain, or even the sense of not belonging with one another, he or she will be driven to do something about it. And that's the key to true empathy. An empathetic person (leader) not only sympathizes with the marginalized person, but he or she tries to do something about it.

These then, are the characteristics of leadership in social equity. While many people in government, business, society, and the military have distinguished themselves by their leadership ability, some have been particularly adept at responding to, and acting on, issues of social equity. Throughout history certain individuals have governed, led, or otherwise caused others to act in the best interests of humanity and they serve now as shining examples of leadership in social equity.

IV. Historical Examples of Leadership in Social Equity

A. Abraham Lincoln

Born in Kentucky, and spending most of his youth and early adulthood in Illinois, Abraham Lincoln developed early a love for learning (on his own) and a gift for telling stories. The former enabled him to begin a successful career in law, and the latter endeared him to his friends and later aided him in seeking several political offices before becoming the sixteenth president of the United States.

Lincoln's love for learning and desire to share his ideas and stories with friends foretold the leadership he was to exhibit later in life. In addition, he recognized in himself at any early age that he was destined for something much greater than his humble beginnings would have suggested, and through hard work and curiosity he took the opportunity to realize his ambitions.

At the same time several incidents in his childhood and early adulthood hinted at an innate sense of fairness and justice that he was developing as he got older.[8] A favorite game of Lincoln's childhood friends was to place hot coals on the backs of turtles to watch them scramble in pain. Lincoln, though, refused to do this, considering it just morally wrong. On another occasion Lincoln was walking along with his friends when they saw a pig literally stuck in the mud and obviously in some distress. He and his friends walked on a bit before Lincoln stopped, and returned to help the animal out of the restricting situation. And when he was eight, he used his father's rifle to kill a wild turkey, as was the custom in providing food for the family. But Lincoln felt so bad in doing this that he vowed to never again kill an animal, even for food. All three instances reveal another side of Lincoln, contrasting with the rough-hewn, calloused, country lawyer.

Lincoln's absolute refusal to give in when he knew he was right was another contributing factor to his developing leadership ability that would stand him well later when he was confronted with the many challenges he experienced in the Civil War. This was evident early on when the General Assembly of the Illinois state legislature voted, along with most other states, to recognize the constitutional right of citizens to own slaves. Even though he was a young legislator, only twenty-six-years-old, he was one of only seven to vote against the measure, which passed by 77 votes. This act was even more noteworthy, given Lincoln's fierce ambition and knowledge that opposing slavery was not necessarily the most politically astute thing he could do. But this vote foretold his mindset when, as president, he had to deal with the very same issue on a scale that precipitated the Civil War.

As president, Lincoln's determination to abolish slavery placed him on the right side of two issues he confronted during his presidency. In both these issues he did not exhibit a passion to end slavery but was completely convinced that it (slavery) was morally wrong, and he had to do everything in his power to end it. This conviction was evident in the first of the two issues regarding slavery that he confronted during his presidency—the Emancipation Proclamation.

While Lincoln began drafting the document in July of 1862, several circumstances delayed its actual signing until several years later.[9] For one, the actual abolition of slavery was still a contentious issue, even in the north. For another, there was the question of to which slaves in the nation the emancipation would apply (just those in the Union, or those living in the Border States which remained in the Union with slavery intact, or even those living in the Confederacy). And in the background of these practical considerations was the issue of the apparent strength of the Union armies to enforce this document, given their less than dominant performance on the battlefield. After several years of personal struggle and, eventually, some significant Union army victories, Lincoln signed the Emancipation Proclamation and it took effect January 1, 1863, though the war continued for more than two years.

The other major issue regarding slavery that confronted Lincoln, and the one that drew from him all his leadership skills, was passage of the thirteenth amendment, which made slavery a violation of the Constitution. While the Senate approved passage of the amendment in 1864, approval by the House was much more difficult, and required the direct involvement of Lincoln in support of a cause in which he deeply believed. Some have even accused him of trading patronage for positive votes in the House, but this, if it occurred, was more a statement of Lincoln's dedication to passage of the amendment than anything to be questioned. Regardless of any political horse trading, the House did approve the amendment in 1865, though tragically ratification by the states came only after his assassination that year.

Both the Emancipation Proclamation and approval of the thirteenth amendment exemplify at least three traits of leadership in social equity on the part of Lincoln. On more than one occasion, he profoundly demonstrated *respect* for all human beings in his concern for the treatment of African Americans. In public addresses he noted often that the practice of slavery was morally wrong, and this contrasted with his sense of *responsibility*, motivating him to do the right thing despite the numerous pressures of the Civil War.

Whether because of, or despite, the many setbacks Lincoln had experienced in his personal life—a less than supportive relationship with his father, the loss of two sons from illness, frequent bouts of depression, a sadness from the loss of life in Union forces—Lincoln displayed a quality of *empathy* not always found in strong leaders.

These leadership traits—respect, responsibility, and empathy—combined to make Abaham Lincoln perhaps the greatest of American presidents, who is best known for his role in ending slavery in this country.

B. Nelson Mandela

Born in 1918 with the expectation of becoming a village chief, Nelson Mandela was initially given the name Rolihlahla ("trouble maker" in the Xhosa language) which, in retrospect, was a harbinger of the life he was to live.[10] Later, his English teacher gave him the more English sounding name "Nelson."[11] But his behavior at an early age reflected his strong sense of the injustice of the apartheid system in South Africa as he became more involved in opposition to the state sponsored treatment of the overwhelmingly black population—so involved that he was thrown out of college for his participation in student protest.

He participated in founding the African National Congress youth league and soon became its president in 1950. He then became one of four deputy presidents in 1952, and was increasingly involved in anti-apartheid protests, which turned violent and led to his arrest for the first time that year. Upon his release from prison, he continued to participate in violent opposition to apartheid until he was arrested again in 1962. Mandela was so committed to the cause that he continued the struggle against apartheid while in prison. He was tried again and sentenced to eighteen more years in prison.

In 1986, while still in prison, he began negotiations with the South African government, and was offered his freedom if he agreed to nonviolence upon his release. But so committed was he to the rights of black South Africans and the end of apartheid, that he refused the offer, and remained in prison until his release in 1990.[12] Between 1990 and 1993, Mandela and the president of South Africa FW De Klerk engaged in negotiations to end South Africa's system of apartheid, for which both men were awarded the Nobel Peace Prize in 1993. Subsequently, in 1994, Mandela was elected the president of the new constitutionally recognized government, ending years of patient resistance to the apartheid system by Mandela, which often turned violent to achieve the aims of the ANC.

Nelson Mandela strove for not only the rights of black South Africans, but for all those who were being unfairly treated by the government and others. In 2005 Mandela's son died of AIDS, and he spoke forcefully for those afflicted by that disease. In his later years, he was also an advocate for the homeless and others suffering from poverty. In 1995 he had founded the Children's Fund to help those affected by these issues.[13]

Indicative of Mandela's leadership in social equity issues was his convening, on his eighty-ninth birthday in 2007, several world leaders dedicated to the same principles of social equity that he had practiced his entire life. The group became known as "The Elders" and included, in addition to Mandela, Archbishop Desmond Tutu, Kofi Annan, President Jimmie Carter, and other world leaders.[14] The Elders, under the leadership of Mandela, has devoted itself to solving many of the world's issues of social equity, including equal rights for women, an end to child marriages, and the advancement of democracy throughout the world.

Almost as a summary of the leadership traits that Mandela embodied throughout his life, *Forbes* magazine presented five strategies which he used to oppose, and then defeat, apartheid in South Africa.[15] The first of these is "Passion Produces Perseverance." Throughout Mandela's life his passion was to achieve equality for the black people of South Africa, and he used this passion to constantly oppose the ruling white government as a student, as a young man, and later as a prisoner for twenty-seven years to persevere until he achieved his goal.

Another lesson Mandela taught us was "Expect Change To Be Messy," and it certainly was through every stage of his life in opposition to apartheid. After his resistance to the white government as a youth and student, he even turned to violent opposition when it seemed that was the only path to change. This of course led to his imprisonment, where, despite incarceration he continued his opposition to apartheid.

Even after living most of his life under the rule of apartheid and experiencing the harsh treatment of twenty-seven years in prison, Mandela believed that "Forgiveness Is Key to Focusing Forward." Upon his release from prison, he was at first understandably angry, but soon realized the cause was more important than the injustice he felt, and he worked with the South African leaders to end apartheid and eventually become the nation's president.

Similarly, Mandela showed the importance of keeping the goal in mind with his constant striving to "End Right vs. Being Right." He knew it was important to realize in his discussions with adversaries that he wouldn't always convince the other side that he was right on every point, if all kept in mind the end goal. His willingness to at least accept the good intentions of others—even when he disagreed with them—enabled him to achieve the ultimate goal: the abolition of apartheid in South Africa. This lesson is especially valuable to leaders seeking to address the many inequities in society, such as racial and religious intolerance. Everyone may not warmly embrace others who believe differently or look different from them, but everyone can accept without reservation others' right to believe differently or look different.

Perhaps the most significant of these leadership lessons from Mandela is his belief—and practice—that "Change Begins from the Inside-Out." If one is to be an agent of change, such as Mandela was in abolishing apartheid, one must know oneself and sincerely believe in the change he or she is seeking to make. And, as seen throughout his life—in his "troublemaking" youth, his later sometimes violent protests against apartheid, his continued work for the cause in prison, and his later discussions with the South African government—Nelson Mandela embodied the change he wished to see.

C. Frederick Douglas

Frederick Douglas was born into slavery in rural Maryland in 1818 and taken from his mother as an infant when she was sent to work on the plantations. He spent his early years with his grandparents, performing domestic chores for their owner until he was six, when he was again separated from his family and sent to work on the plantation under the harshest conditions.[16.] It was during this period in which he learned what it meant to be treated less than humanly, performing the hardest physical work, and driven almost to starvation by the slave owner. Fortunately, when he was eight, his owner sent him to live with another owner in Baltimore where conditions were much more humane and younger Frederick helped in raising the owner's natural children.

One of the things he did during this time was listen to the slave owner's wife read from the Bible to her own child while Frederick listened, fascinated by the written word. When he tried to learn to read himself the wife's husband saw this and was furious that a slave could be learning to read. Frederick was only more fascinated by the ability to read, thinking—correctly—that the owner was afraid that his slaves could become more independent by becoming literate. This realization made him even more determined to learn to read and write, and he took every opportunity to educate himself—listening to scripture being read, seeing words in print, and learning the alphabet. A particularly noteworthy event was when he got a copy of *Noah Webster's American Spelling Book*, which he took every opportunity to master. He continued looking for ways to practice the alphabet and sound out various words between the menial tasks of a house slave.

In his constant search for ways to improve his ability to write and speak, Frederick found a copy of *The Columbus Orator*, which contained the speeches of famous men throughout history. He read them with fascination and practiced them over and over, sounding them aloud to absorb the lessons they taught. As he learned about the achievements of these great men and witnessed the inhuman conditions of the slave trade on the Baltimore docks, he became more and more aware of the pain and stark injustice inflicted on African Americans.

When he was fourteen his original owner brought him back to rural Maryland where the living and working conditions were much more brutal than in Baltimore. As was the custom, his owner lent him out to another farmer who had a reputation for severely mistreating his slaves. Frederick bristled under this treatment and even came to blows with the owner until he was again sent to live with another slave owner where the conditions were somewhat better. Still, he continued to educate himself and became more aware of the power of knowing how to read and write, and the cruelty and stark inequity with which African American slaves in nineteenth century America were treated. Eventually, he made up his mind to escape slavery and set off for New Bedford, Massachusetts, when he was twenty-one.

Finding work in New Bedford, Frederick came across a copy of *The Liberator*, the newspaper founded and operated by the abolitionist William Lloyd Garrison. Both the newspaper and its founder had a profound influence on Douglas, especially the way in which Garrison awakened in him the moral aspect of slavery, fanning the flames of injustice that he already felt. He also learned at this time that the Constitution effectively legitimized the institution of slavery in its Article 1, Section 2, which provided for counting a slave as three-fifths of a person in determining Congressional representation. Douglas, having experienced the humiliation and pain of slavery in his own life, now became a vocal part of the growing abolitionist movement.

As Douglas took every opportunity to speak at events, he grew more and more passionate about abolition, and he drew the attention of everyone hearing him speak. After achieving the notice of Garrison and others in the abolition movement he was given the opportunity to speak at the Massachusetts Antislavery Society annual convention and he was a huge success. This was the result of a sincere conviction that slavery was morally wrong and years of practice sounding out words for their maximum effect. His reputation as an effective abolitionist spread throughout the northern states, and even in England where slavery was considered wrong.

Frederick Douglas was becoming so highly regarded as an abolitionist that many doubted his sincerity, since such an articulate spokesman could not have lived the life of a slave. In response, he wrote the *Narrative of the Life of Frederick Douglas, an American Slave* in 1845, which only enhanced his reputation as an abolitionist. The book was widely acclaimed not only in the Union, but in England as well, where he visited and spread word on the abolitionist cause. Later, in 1855, he wrote *My Bondage and My Freedom* of which three editions were published, and which confirmed him as a role model for other African American slaves seeking their freedom.

At first, Douglas was not convinced of Abraham Lincoln's authentic opposition to slavery, but his (Lincoln's) Emancipation Proclamation, changed that. Douglas soon developed a bond with Lincoln and became an influence on Lincoln's prosecution of the Civil War, and the passage of the thirteenth amendment, which would make slavery unconstitutional throughout the country.

Later, Douglas extended his opposition to slavery to include suffrage, and he influenced passage of the fifteenth amendment which gave African American men the right to vote. In his final years he devoted himself to writing and speaking about women's rights, which affirmed his leadership in social equity.

D. Ruth Bader Ginsburg

Ruth Bader Ginsburg was born and raised in a neighborhood of mixed ethnicity in Brooklyn, and she grew up seeing no difference in the personal worth of the different nationalities and beliefs of her neighbors. But one of her earliest memories of seeing such differences was seeing a sign, while traveling in Pennsylvania, on a bed and breakfast that said NO DOGS OR JEWS ALLOWED.[17]

And this may have left an impression on her of the need for someone to speak up for people who are the victims of discrimination but are either unwilling or unable to speak up for themselves.

One of the strongest influences on Kiki, as Ruth was then known, was that of her mother, Celia, who had the highest expectations for her daughter. Herself a child of the depression, Celia saved all that she could for Ruth's education and constantly emphasized to her the importance of doing her best in school. Unfortunately, Celia became ill while Ruth was in high school and passed away before her daughters' graduation. Fortunately, though, she did live to see Kiki accepted by Cornell University. Ironically, Celia's death taught Kiki a lesson in justice which would stay with her. At Celia's mourning observance, Kiki, being a young woman, could not be in included in the *minyan*, or Jewish prayer observance for the dead, because only men could be counted. This, for Ruth, was the ultimate injustice, given her devotion to her mother, and the lesson would probably remain in her later fight for women's rights.

Another strong influence on Ruth occurred during her senior year at Cornell. It was during the McCarthy era, and his Permanent Subcommittee on Investigations in Congress called Marcus Singer, a professor of zoology at Cornell, before the Senate committee for his refusal to name another professor supposedly involved in Marxist activities. The Cornell student body erupted in anger over this event, and it awakened in Ruth a desire to practice law in hopes of opposing such an injustice in the future. More generally, she viewed the practice of law as "something good for your society."[18] After Cornell, she was accepted at Harvard Law School, but had to re-apply and be reaccepted due to her husband's military service. At Harvard she began to distinguish herself, becoming one of only two women on the Law Review.

As a young woman, she encountered the first discrimination against women in the workplace as she sought employment as an attorney. After completing Harvard Law School, she was repeatedly disappointed to find many of the positions at law firms were open only to men before she was able to join the law school faculty at Rutgers. While there she was able to draw on her observations on, and experiences of, the treatment of women in society by founding the Women's Rights Project. Later, she became the first tenured woman on the Columbia Law School faculty in 1972, and it was here that she began to concentrate on sex discrimination cases. Also, it was here that she began to develop a strategy of *incrementalism*, choosing her battles carefully, and being satisfied with small victories to build a reservoir of achievement in advancing gender equality.

Ironically, it was also at this time that she demonstrated that gender equality worked both ways. Social mores sometimes treated men unfairly also, in that men were often denied the same benefits as women, simply because they were male. In *Weinberger v. Wiesenfeld* in 1975 she recognized the injustice of denying social security benefits to a widower simply because it was the usual case for a woman to rely on a husband's income and was therefore entitled to benefits upon his death. But in this case, Stephen Wiesenfeld was the primary caregiver for his family while his wife worked as a schoolteacher, and, when she died unexpectedly he applied for survivor's benefits. Upon denial of these benefits, Ginsburg fought to ensure that he received them, and won, signaling that her passion on the Women's Rights Project flowed not just from her position as a woman, but rather from her fervent belief in justice.

Yet, her strongest belief was in addressing the unjust treatment of women in the workplace, and society in general, not just because of its unfairness to women, but because she believed that society would benefit by their equal treatment. In this regard she once stated that, men need the experience of working with women who demonstrate a wide range of personality characteristics, they need to become working friends with women.[19]

In 1980, Jimmie Carter appointed Ruth Bader Ginsburg to the U.S. Court of Appeals for the District of Columbia, in which position she began to moderate her natural inclinations as a passionate spokesperson for women. This was partly due, probably, to her realization that she could accomplish more through a moderate approach, but also since the Court of Appeals consists of three judges, and compromise was essential to successful decisions.

Her tenure on the Court of Appeals did not go unnoticed, and in 1993 President Bill Clinton nominated her to the U.S. Supreme Court, finally providing another women's voice, in addition to that of Sandra Day O'Conner. Over the next several years, she either wrote the majority opinion in decisions finding in favor of some women's rights issue or the minority opinion in such cases decided not so favorably for women. Among those winning was the case in 1996 which decided in favor of women to attend the previously all-male Virginia Military Institute (VMI). But even when she wrote the dissenting opinion as she did in the Lily Ledbetter decision in which the issue of equal pay for women gained universal attention, she was passionate in achieving the fair treatment of women. But she was also just as passionate in all cases of injustice as she showed in writing the dissenting opinion in the defeat of a key part of the Voting Rights Act in 2013. At the same time, she has consistently foiled numerous attempts to overthrow *Roe v. Wade*, the landmark decision to protect a women's right to choose to terminate a pregnancy.

Throughout her long stay on the Supreme Court, Justice Ginsburg has provided leadership in protecting the rights of women, and she has proven to be its conscience in all issues of social justice. The fact that she has done this through numerous challenges to her health only enhances the esteem with which she is held by her colleagues and all those for whom she has fought for social justice.

E. Franklin Delano Roosevelt

Franklin Delano Roosevelt, often referred to as just "FDR," the thirty-second president of the United States, had what most would call a privileged childhood, enjoying sports and outdoor games with his father, and stamp collecting and other more sedate indoor activities with his mother. As he was an only child, both his parents doted on him and spent a lot of constructive time with him, and this probably influenced his love of people and his very sociable nature and his ability to work toward common goals with others. Unfortunately, his father suffered a severe heart attack when Franklin was only eight and this curtailed the many outdoor activities with his father, but it also provided the first experience at readjustment that he would need later in life.

When he was fourteen Franklin again had to readjust to life's circumstances when he left for boarding school and both he and his mother missed the mutual support system they developed with his father's illness. Even though he had a hard time fitting in, he always sent optimistic letters home and maintained a positive outlook, a trait which was to stand him in good stead later in life. He did find encouragement from his participation on the debate team in which he excelled due to thorough preparation and often consulting with his father on ways to perfect his delivery. Other than his participation on the debate team, he showed little excellence in any of his academic subjects. In fact, his only real ambition was to grow up "to be like his father, straight and honorable, just and kind, an upstanding American."[20]

The impact of his father's death from a heart attack during Franklin's first semester at Harvard can only be imagined. But, as was his custom, Franklin adjusted to this loss and discovered his love for journalism when he joined the staff of the student newspaper, *The Harvard Crimson*. So taken was he by communicating with the public (the Harvard newspaper is the only one in the City of Cambridge) that he rapidly rose through staff positions until he became its Editor in Chief. It was probably during this ascent through leadership positions at the paper that he developed many of his interpersonal skills and discovered the importance and satisfaction of public service. Later in life he would look back on this first position of leadership as one that helped to prepare him for other leadership challenges he would face.

Another significant event in his development as both a person and leader was his meeting, and falling in love with, Eleanor Roosevelt, who introduced Franklin to an entirely different way of viewing his relationships with other human beings. She was at that time considered what would be known today as a Progressive or Liberal, and her outlook in helping others had a profound effect on Franklin then and in the coming years. In one particular incident during their courtship Franklin accompanied her on one of her many charitable pursuits when she accompanied a sick child home. He must have been struck by his growing love for her shown by this selfless act, and the act itself which demonstrated the care of one human being for another. It can only be surmised the effect this had on Franklin later in life as he made decisions to improve the welfare of others.

As he grew older, two characteristics of his early childhood and growth as a young man appeared to have a strong influence on this developing leadership ability. One, from an early age he had a strong, but different relationship with both his parents. Until his father's illness he had enjoyed many outdoor activities with him, and these experiences probably instilled a confidence born of a strong father-son relationship. But he enjoyed an equally strong relationship with his mother, who instilled in him an enjoyment of indoor activities such as stamp collecting. In both cases, however, Franklin, as an only child, sought always to please both parents in their separate activities.

The second quality he displayed at an early age, and maintained throughout his life, was an ever-present optimism in the face of life's challenges. This sustained him emotionally during both the onset of his father's illness, and, later, when his father died while Franklin was in his first year at Harvard. It can only be surmised how valuable this ever-present optimism would be as he faced his own serious illness, and later, during the challenges of the Great Depression and World War II.

As he began his life with Eleanor, he developed an affinity for politics, driven probably by a growing social conscience influenced by his wife. Another contributing factor was probably his name recognition as the fifth cousin of President Theodore Roosevelt in being elected a state senator from New York. In this position he soon found himself at odds with the existing Tammany Hall political machine, and he learned well the art of compromise and moderation in helping to achieve the Progressive goals popular with the working class (a shorter work week, workman's compensation, and women's suffrage). So well did he adapt to these meaningful causes that President Wilson appointed him to a position he had long sought—Assistant Secretary of the Navy—in which he excelled at the interpersonal and organization skills developed earlier.

Unfortunately, personal tragedy struck in 1921 when FDR contracted what was eventually diagnosed as polio. Stricken at first by the realization that he'd no longer be able to participate in his favorite outdoor activities, he then used his long developed personal optimism to pursue numerous exercises and remedies that he hoped would restore his mobility. Among these was the time spent nurturing his health at Warm Springs, Georgia, which was doubly beneficial to him. One, the therapeutic power of the waters gave him some comfort as he sought a more permanent healing of his condition. But, probably of greater significance was his developing relationships with the other afflicted persons undergoing treatment at Warm Springs. In addition to the effect Eleanor and her strong social conscience and activities had on Franklin, he soon developed a new appreciation for those experiencing the same physical hardships as he, and he used his already developed organizational skills to transform Warm Springs into a truly effective rehabilitation center. At Warm Springs he also underwent what is today recognized as a total "spiritual transformation" resulting from his complete acceptance of his physical impairment and the close relationship he had with others at the center.[21]

Several years later Al Smith asked Franklin to nominate him for president at the Democratic Convention. By this time Franklin was in a wheelchair and very visibly handicapped, and he struggled over the decision to do so. On the one hand he was still very captivated by a political life and the desire to accomplish things for those less fortunate, such as the other physically handicapped friendships he had made at Warm Springs. On the other hand, he was concerned about the image he would present in his severely handicapped state at the Convention. FDR decided to give the speech which he delivered with such passion and conviction that, arguably, he entered a new stage of his political life. This decision to present himself to the American people as he was, was similar to the courage he was to exhibit in the coming years of the Depression and World War II.

Yet it would be almost four years before he returned to politics to become the Governor of New York. During these four years he threw himself into working with a passion to develop Warm Springs, so much so, that he became known as "old Doc Roosevelt, "head counselor, spiritual director, and Vice-President in charge of picnics."[22] Over this period he developed a warm relationship with all those at Warm Springs afflicted with diseases like his. It can only be assumed that this involvement with Warm Springs and its residents prepared him well for the leadership role he was to fulfill later in his advocacy for the disabled.

Again, it was Al Smith who provided Roosevelt with the encouragement to run for Governor of New York, which he did, in spite of his physical condition. After winning the office, he reflected the personal inclinations of Eleanor for the downtrodden in society, and his own political experience and period of recovery at Warm Springs to become the nation's greatest advocate for the common man. It was this firm conviction that his state government owed relief to those most affected by the Great Depression, which he ensured through tax and other public policy initiatives in New York. So successful was he at doing this that New York became the model for other states in the throes of the Great Depression.

It was of little surprise then, that the Democratic National Convention nominated him for president in 1932, an office he was to hold until his death in 1945. In characteristic fashion he began his first term with a 100-day program specifically designed to help the common man weather the Great Depression. And he marked the start of this effort by inspiring the country with his now famous "the only thing we have to *fear* is . . . *fear* itself."

Included in this 100-day program was creation of the Civilian Conservation Corps (CCC), which was envisioned to provide much needed employment to 250,000 Americans but ultimately became two and a half million unemployed.[23] In addition to providing much needed employment to many Americans, the CCC had the unifying benefit of bringing together men and women from different areas of the country bound by a common purpose (recovering from the Great Depression). It was at this time that FDR sought to bring meaningful work to the common men and women of the U.S. by establishing the Public Works Administration and Works Progress Administration. It can only be assumed that, in addition to drawing upon his natural inclination to help those in need, he was able to call upon the skills learned at Warm Springs to create organizations which would help those less fortunate than he through participation in their own recovery.

Possibly the act of leadership in social equity for which FDR is best known was creation of the Social Security Act of 1935. It's almost hard to imagine a society in which millions grew old without any means of support, or experienced health or accident catastrophes without the ability to care for themselves or passed away with dependents without any means of support, but these were common occurrences during the Great Depression. Fortunately, FDR recognized the need to address these needs in American society, and saw, correctly, the ability of Social Security, later amended to include Medicare in 1965, to provide relief to Americans in need.

Arguably, no other president has done as much to advance the cause of social equity in government as FDR.

F. Harriet Tubman

Harriet Tubman was born into slavery in Maryland in 1820, although there is some question as to the actual year. What is known is that, as a slave, she was responsible for many domestic and farming tasks typically assigned to a young girl by the slave owner. Among the first tasks assigned by her owner was that of caring for an infant although she herself was only a five-year-old little girl. This may have helped prepare her for the leadership responsibilities she was to assume later in life.

Another circumstance which may have reflected her attitude toward slavery and influenced her passion to helping other slaves occurred when she was twelve years old in a grocery store. A slave owner had just mistreated one of his slaves who proceeded to run away. Harriet stood between the slave owner and runaway slave, which infuriated the slave owner, who threw a heavy metal object at the escaping slave. The metal weight missed the slave, but struck Harriet in the head, leaving a deep gash and injury which affected her the rest of her life. From then on she would experience frequent headaches, uncontrollable sleeping spells, and hallucinations, which she would interpret as religious apparitions. It can only be conjectured the influence this incident and physical disability had on Harriet in her desire to help other slaves, but she interpreted the visions she had as a sign that she was destined to help others gain their freedom.

While she never learned to read and write, the many tasks Harriet had to perform including cooking, laundering clothing, caring for the sick, and working in the fields prepared her well for her later life. As she labored in the countryside at different locations she became familiar with the landscape and how to survive under the harsh treatment of her owners. She was able to escape and survive using the many skills she had acquired. Eventually, she put her skills to work on the "Underground Railroad," helping escaping slaves in South Carolina and other southern states make their way north to Canada. Among the many survival skills she had attained was a sense of direction, helping others find their way north using the North Star. In all, she made nineteen trips helping other slaves find their freedom on the Underground Railroad. So inspirational was she in helping these slaves find their promised land that she became known as their Moses.[24]

Harriet used these same skills serving as one of the first African Americans to serve with the Union Army as a nurse, cook, guide, and even spy. She was influential in recruiting other African Americans to fight against the Confederacy, and she guided 150 black soldiers in the Combahee River Raid which gave 750 slaves their freedom.[25] What probably stands out most about Harriet's leadership is that she provided not only inspiration for the escaping slaves, but she personally arranged for their physical care in providing food and housing, often with her own meager financial resources.

After the war she returned home to Auburn, New York, where she welcomed the poor into her home, and fed them even though she herself was poor. She also became a strong supporter of the Women's Rights Movement, traveling extensively in Boston, New York, and Philadelphia, where she spoke and organized for that cause. Harriet Tubman left her mark as a leader in providing a better life for not only those escaping slavery but for anyone seeking food and shelter, poor as she was. She was especially concerned about the welfare of the elderly poor, and raised funds to purchase twenty-five acres next to her home on which she established a home for the elderly.

In so many areas of human need—helping escaping slaves in the Underground Railroad, working for women's rights, and tending to the needs of the elderly poor—Harriet Tubman was a beacon of leadership for those needing it most.

G. Dietrich Bonhoeffer

Born February 4, 1906, as one of eight children into a well-educated family—his father was a well-known German psychiatrist and his mother a teacher—his family expected young Deitrich to pursue some similar profession. However, his interests turned early in life to theology, and he received his Doctor of Theology in 1927.

Still not old enough to be ordained a minister, he visited the United States in 1930 where he was greatly disturbed to see the extent of racial discrimination in that country—a revelation that he came to compare with the anti-Semitism in Germany. While there Bonhoeffer learned two significant lessons which were to stay with him throughout his work as a minister in Germany.[26] One was the fact that the mark of a true leader was having an impact on peoples' lives, again a lesson which, it can only be assumed, was of immense value to him in his later work. The other related lesson learned in America, stemming from the social conditions he observed in New York, was the importance of empathy in his work as a minister.

Bonhoeffer returned to Germany in 1931 and was ordained a Protestant priest. He soon became critical of the newly elected Chancellor Adolf Hitler for his anti-Semitism and interference in the church, and he even made a radio broadcast critical of the German peoples' acceptance of the new leader's religious views.

In 1933 Bonhoeffer visited the Bethel, which was a community dedicated to housing the physically and mentally afflicted.[27] This visit had a lasting effect on Bonhoeffer for at least three reasons. One, especially given his somewhat privileged background, he was exposed to what real suffering is, and this probably contributed to his empathy for disadvantaged and otherwise poorly treated human beings. Secondly, he now saw firsthand the importance of Christian care in relieving the suffering of such human beings. He related the treatment of these severely afflicted human beings to some of the inhumane practices of the Nazis, such as euthanasia. In this regard he found the treatment of non-Aryans, especially the Jews, abhorrent for such practices as banning them from civil service positions, although this treatment was to become much worse in the years to come.

Probably with such thoughts in mind he worked with the German Evangelical Church and wrote in 1933 *The Church and the Jewish Question* which questioned the legality of state interference in Church matters. In this document he called upon the church to address three issues.[28] One, it said the church should call upon the state to explain why it could interfere in the affairs of the church. Two, the church should respond to the call for it (the church) to care for those being persecuted. And three, the church should publicly hold the state responsible for this persecution. About the same time he pressed the German Evangelical Church to renounce the State's Aryan Paragraph, the Nazi regulation which prohibited Jews "from becoming members in German economic establishments, political parties, social clubs, volunteer organizations, student groups, sports groups, and other institutions."[29] Unfortunately, Bonhoeffer was in a small minority that expressed such opposition to the state for its treatment of the Jews. These were among the earliest signs of the courageous leadership Bonhoeffer displayed in his concern for those persecuted by the Nazis.

At the beginning of 1935 he became director of a school at Finkenwalde which trained seminarians in the new Confessing Church which opposed the state supported German protestant church. The seminary's teaching was based on Christ's Sermon on the Mount, and, as such, it emphasized community and its responsibility to care for others as called for in scripture. However, the Reich (German state) soon grew intolerant with both the Confessing Church, which it declared illegal, and Finkenwalde, which it closed in 1935.

Bonhoeffer continued his ministerial work in the Confessing Church, preaching his care for those persecuted by the Third Reich, while watching with horror as the German state continued its march through Europe and persecution of the Jewish people. In late 1940 Bonhoeffer's brother-in-law secured a position for him in the *Abwehr*, which was the German intelligence agency. Bonhoeffer was able to use his many religious contacts throughout Europe to supposedly gather intelligence for the German Nazi government, when in reality he was working against the Third Reich. These efforts resulted in Bonhoeffer helping a number of Jewish people to flee the country and avoid extermination.

It should be noted that Bonhoeffer, being a Christian and leader in his faith, did consider the morality of assassinating Hitler, but concluded that it wasn't immoral to do so. For him it would have been wrong to do nothing in the face of such evil. The most important thing for Bonhoeffer was to help those suffering in Germany at the hands of this tyrant.

Eventually, however, Hitler learned the origin of the several attempts on his life, and Bonhoeffer was implicated. He was sent to Tegel Prison in 1943 where he maintained his strong faith in the face of his imprisonment and interrogations. It is said that even during these interrogations his interrogators sensed his strong presence as a leader, even in prison. He maintained this outlook and abiding concern for his fellow prisoners until he was hanged in 1943.

Bonhoeffer's legacy is one primarily as a minister in his care for others, especially the unfortunate and those persecuted by Hitler in his attempt to exterminate the Jews. He leaves various writings, especially those completed while in prison, and he is especially known for *The Cost of Discipleship*, published in 1937, and his well-known *Ethics*, begun while he was in prison, but not published until 1955.

Also, his thoughts on "religionless Christianity" are somewhat unique to Bonhoeffer in that he considered good works and helping the less fortunate as the hallmark of a good Christian. Perhaps most important though, in the years following his death, was his influence on future social movements such as the resistance to Apartheid in South Africa.

H. Martin Luther King Jr.

Born Michael King Jr. January 15, 1929, he had his name changed to Martin Luther King, Jr., when he was six, after his father became Martin Luther King, Sr. His father was descended from a family of sharecroppers, but his maternal grandfather had been a minister who eventually became head of the Ebenezer Baptist church in Atlanta. When he (his grandfather) died his father became pastor of that church and impressed upon Martin Jr. his belief that racism and segregation were offenses against God and the importance of using Christianity to oppose them.[30]

Being very bright, he entered Morehouse College at fifteen. But he was not drawn to the ministry until he attended a bible class in his junior year when he decided to become a minister, following in the footsteps of this father and grandfather.

At Morehouse he became student body president, and then attended Crozer Theological Seminary in Pennsylvania, where he excelled, becoming the class valedictorian. While in the seminary Morehouse president Benjamin E. Hayes, a vehement advocate for racial equality, inspired King to devote himself in this endeavor through Christianity.

After leaving the seminary King accepted a position as Pastor of the Dexter Avenue Baptist church in Montgomery in 1954, and a year later received his PhD from Boston University.

In December of 1955 Rosa Parks, a young African American woman, sitting in the "colored" section of the bus, refused to give up her seat to a white man when all the seats in the white section were taken. She was arrested, found in violation of the Montgomery City Code, and fined for her violation, which enflamed the local chapter of the NAACP. Local leaders looked to King, even though he was only twenty-six at the time, for guidance in protesting Parks' arrest. He was appointed President of the Montgomery Improvement Association, beginning what was to become a lifelong devotion to non-violent activism for racial equality.

Under his leadership, the local African American population began a 382-day boycott of the bus system which eventually led to the U.S. Supreme Court ruling that bus segregation was unconstitutional. What was more important, though, was the fact that the boycott drew the attention of the entire country and showed what could be achieved through non-violent means. But for King, who was suddenly thrust into a leadership role, the boycott revealed to him five lessons that were to mark his ascendance to that role. First, it was obvious, given the wide disparity between the white and black communities of Montgomery, that a unifying voice was needed. Secondly, he became aware that, young as he was, he would have to become familiar with the workings of an organization. Thirdly, given his natural propensity for public speaking, he would have to act as the organization's spokesman. Fourth, and related to his role as spokesperson, he would probably become a symbol of the movement. Finally, he was convinced of the need to establish relationships with all sides on the issues of racism and desegregation.

The 382-day boycott was successful, and this established King's reputation as a leader nationally in advocating for civil rights, especially through non-violent means.

Building on the success of the boycott, in 1957 King became the president of the Southern Christian Leadership Conference, firmly establishing him as the voice of African American opposition to racism. Considering the voting process key to this opposition, the Conference directed its attention to securing voting rights for African Americans. Under King's leadership, in February of 1958 it organized twenty mass meetings in southern cities to address this issue.

Early in 1960 King encouraged students to use nonviolence in lunch counter sit-ins to press their cause for equal treatment with whites, which eventually led to establishing the Student Nonviolent Coordinating Committee (SNCC). Later that year he joined seventy-five students requesting service at an Atlanta department store lunch counter. When they were denied service, they refused to leave, and thirty-six of them, including King, were arrested. The incident drew the attention of President John F. Kennedy, who intervened and eventually secured King's release.

In early 1963 King arranged a demonstration in the city of Birmingham which involved local families. When the police trained dogs and firehoses on the crowds, King was criticized for including families with children. He was jailed for organizing and participating in the demonstration, and it was while in jail that he wrote his famed *Letter from a Birmingham Jail*, which explained his belief in nonviolence to achieve the aims of racial equality. The letter received national attention and added to the growing perception of King as the symbol of the movement toward racial equality.

In August of 1963 King organized the March on Washington in which 200,000 participated, and it was before the Lincoln Memorial that he presented his famous *I have a dream* speech. The speech captivated the country then, and continues to do so now, as representative of King's philosophy of using nonviolence to achieve the aims of racial equality. It also led to passage of the Civil Rights Act of 1964 and probably King's selection for the Noble Peace Prize of 1964.

After several marches from Selma to Montgomery were either canceled or interrupted by police using tear gas and nightsticks, another one in which 25,000 participated, ended at the state capital. This once again drew the attention of President Lyndon Johnson who used the power of his office to secure passage of the Voting Rights Act of 1965. This legislation led to a huge increase in the registration of African American voters and the subsequent elections of numerous African Americans to political office.[30]

In the period from 1965 to 1967 King spread his message of nonviolent protest throughout the country, adding opposition to the Vietnam War to his message of racial equality, especially since a disproportionate number of African Americans and poor were having to participate in that war.

King's legacy as a leader in social equity, especially in racial equality, is due to his emphasis on nonviolence as the only effective way to advance racial equity. King maintained this resolve in the face of the opposition by many of his own race who were eager to use violence to achieve racial equality. This only demonstrated the importance of his leadership in striving to achieve racial equality through legislation and peaceful demonstration.

I. Malala Yousafzai

Malala Yousafzai was born July 12, 1997 in Mingora, located in the Swat Valley of Pakistan, a picturesque region popular with tourists. Her family named her Malala after Malalai, who was known as Afghanistan's Joan of Arc because of her role in fighting the British in 1880.[31] She attended the school founded by her father Ziauddin Yousafzai, who was a social activist and educator. But in 2007 the Taliban, which considered education contrary to its beliefs, especially that for young girls, attacked the school. This prompted the statement by Malala in 2008, which, even at the age of eleven, displayed her passion for education and fierce activism in its cause, "How dare the Taliban take away my basic right to education."[32]

Unquestionably, the seeds of Malala's activism and leadership, even at an early age, were sown by her father, himself an activist in the cause of education, who provided the inspiration and guidance for her activities. But her genuine belief in the value of education for improving the lives of young people, especially girls, undoubtedly drove her to constantly fight for it as a universal right. Finally, though, the very act of the Taliban's persecution against a cause in which she so fervently believed, probably drove her to literally heroic activities in its defense.

Among these early activities was the blog on the Taliban treatment of girls she wrote for the BBC in 2009 under the pen name Gul Maki. It's important to remember that this was after the Taliban had attacked her school, yet she continued to speak regularly on the right of girls to receive an education, and otherwise act in opposition to the Taliban. As a result of these activities Desmond Tutu nominated her for the International Children's Peace Prize and she received the Pakistan Children's Peace Prize in 2011.

Malala continued her fierce opposition to the Taliban until one day in 2012 when she was on her way home from school one of the terrorists boarded the bus she was riding and shot her in the head. So serious was her injury, that her family sent her to Birmingham, England, for treatment and the continuance of her education.

The event drew national and worldwide attention, and the UN envoy on global education formalized the call for all the world's children to receive an education. It also resulted in Pakistan passing its first Right to Education law, and it established a $10 million fund in Malala's name.

In 2013, when she was only sixteen, Malala formally appealed to world leaders to address education and women's rights. This appeal also included her plea for world leaders to put an end to poverty, illiteracy, and terrorism. As a result, UN Secretary General Ban Ki-moon formally dedicated July 12—her birthday—as "Malala Day." It's particularly noteworthy that she achieved these advances in human rights when she was herself little more than a child.

Recognizing these achievements, and her belief in the power of the individual to bring about change in society, the European Parliament in 2013 bestowed on her the Sakharov Prize for Freedom of Thought. In 2014 she became the youngest person ever to win the Nobel Peace Prize, and three years later the UN named her its Messenger of Peace to carry forth its message in support of girls' education.

Probably Malala's most significant legacy is the inspiration she's provided others, especially young girls and women, at a very early age. The courage she displayed in speaking out against the Taliban for something in which she believed, particularly as a child, is nothing short of amazing; then, to continue doing so after being seriously wounded by terrorists shows a stubborn resilience that all of us can envy.

Almost forgotten among her many achievements is the extensive writing she pursued, in addition to the blog she did for the BBC mentioned earlier. By the age of twenty-one she had already published several books, among which were *I Am Malala, Malala's Magic Pencil,* and *We Are Displaced: My Journey* and *Stories from Refugee Girls Around the World.*

And then there's the Malala Fund which she established with her father, and which seeks to make available twelve years of education to girls everywhere. While the goal is worldwide, the fund focuses especially on countries where educational opportunities for young girls are most urgent, such as Pakistan, Afghanistan, the Sudan, and sub-Saharan Africa.

While the main emphasis of Malala's work has been girls' education, she has devoted increasing effort to addressing poverty, illiteracy, and human rights throughout the world. Especially for these efforts she has made an extensive contribution to leadership in social equity.

J. Pope Francis

Jorge Mario Bergoglio was born in Buenos Aires on December 17, 1936, of Italian parents. His father having emigrated from Italy and, as a result, he spoke both Italian and Spanish. At an early age he developed a love of science, even before he decided to enter the priesthood, and he received a degree in chemistry from the University of Buenos Aires. But at the same time, he grew up with a strong sense of social justice, influenced probably by Juan Peron, the president of Argentina at the time, himself an advocate for the poor in Buenos Aires.[33] After a struggle with how to go forward in life, he entered the priesthood at age twenty-one, and became a Jesuit priest in 1969.

After ordination, he followed a path of social justice, typical of the philosophy of the Jesuit order, and he advanced rapidly, eventually becoming the leader of Argentinian Jesuits at the age of thirty-six. This was the time of violent political upheaval in Argentina, a period known as the "Dirty War" in which people practicing their faith, including Jesuits, were persecuted, even to the extent of being murdered. Many Jesuits claimed that Bergoglio was not doing enough in their defense, and the order was divided into pro- and anti-Bergoglio groups.[34] Opposition to Bergoglio was so great that the anti-Bergoglio groups succeeded in having him banished into a two-year exile away from the Order. It was during this time that he probably had an opportunity to examine his theology that sustained him in the future.

Fortunately, he had an ally in the new bishop of Buenos Aires, Antonio Quarracino, who selected Bergoglio as an auxiliary bishop in 1992. Six years later, upon the death of Quarracino, he became archbishop of Buenos Aires, and three years later was named a cardinal by Pope John Paul II.

It is noteworthy that, even though he was considered conservative by other Jesuits, there are identifiable reasons for which he became more and more progressive, especially regarding issues affecting the poor.[35] For one thing, there was severe poverty in Argentina at the time, and, especially as a Jesuit, this had to occupy his thoughts and work as a spiritual leader. Secondly, after Peron, the fascist government of Argentina had to have had a contrary effect on him, in terms of his own progressivism. Also, even during his earlier, somewhat conservative years in the priesthood, he had always been a populist, driven probably by his background as a Jesuit. Finally, he had always been supported by a more liberal branch of the College of Cardinals. For these reasons, it is not surprising that he became such an advocate for the poor and disadvantaged when he acceded to the Papacy in 2013 and took the name Francis from Saint Francis of Assisi who himself had a special attachment to the poor.

Almost immediately he showed connection and empathy to the common person and those who were poor or otherwise different from him. Rather than live in the ornate Papal residence, he moved into a simple apartment in the Vatican. And in response to a question about the morality of homosexuality his response was "Who am I to judge?"[36]

He also spoke forcefully on the war in Syria that September, leading a special vigil in St. Peter's square which 100,000 people attended. And in December he provided his thoughts on what the Catholic Church should be, when he said "I prefer a Church which is bruised, hurting, and dirty, because it has been out on the streets."[37]

In 2014 he was nominated for the Nobel Peace Prize, and he continued to speak out against corrupt governments and their treatment of their citizens. On issues of immigration, he came to the defense of people fleeing these governments seeking a better life. So vocal was his criticism of those taking advantage of the poor and powerless that he himself received death threats.[38]

But perhaps the achievement regarding social equity for which he will be best known is his May 2015 encyclical *PRAISE TO YOU (Laudato Si') On Care for Our Common Home*. While that encyclical is probably best known for its environmental message, especially on climate change, it emphasizes equally Pope Francs' concern for the poor, including the reminder to remember them in all that we do.

In 2017 Pope Francis visited both Myanmar and Bangladesh for discussions with the leaders of both countries to address the treatment of their citizens, especially refugees, solidifying his reputation of concern for the poor and disadvantaged.

In addition to *Laudato Si'*, Pope Francis's message of social justice may be best illustrated in the 2018 film *Pope Francis: A Man of His Word*, which was shown at the Cannes Film Festival that year. That film probably best covers the many issues of social justice, including poverty, excessive attachment to material things, wealth inequality, and immigration for which he will be long remembered.

References

1. Scott Shafer, *40 Years After The Assassination Of Harvey Milk, LGBTQ Candidates Find Success*, NPR, November 27, 2018.
2. Prudy Gourguechon, *Empathy Is An Essential Leadership Skill—And There's Nothing Soft About It*, Forbes, December 26, 2017.
3. H. George Frederickson, *The State of Social Equity in American Public Administration*, National Civic Review, Winter, 2005.
4. *Remembering the Legacy* AFRICAN AMERICANS IN THE MILITARY, June 30, 2015.
5. Trevor Nace, *New Survey Finds 3 Out Of 4 Americans Accept The Reality Of Climate Change*, Forbes, January 23, 2019.
6. Katharine Hayhoe, *Five myths about climate change*, Washington Post.
7. Robert Gilleskie, LIGHTING THE WAY *Providing Leadership in Sustainable Development*, Mill City Press, 2018.
8. Doris Kearns Goodwin, LEADERSHIP IN TURBULENT TIMES, Simon & Shuster, 2018.
9. Nancy Koehn, FORGED IN CRISIS THE POWER OF COURAGEOUS LEADERSHIP IN TURBULENT TIMES, Scribner, 2017.

10. Richard Stengel, *Mandela: His 8 Lessons of Leadership*, TIME, July 9, 2008.
11. *Nelson Mandela—Leadership Which Ended Apartheid*, BUSINESS & LEADERSHIP, July 30, 2018.
12. Amy Costello, *Nelson Mandela, the man who brought South Africa out of apartheid, dies at 95*, PRI's The World, December 5, 2013.
13. Brand South Africa Reporter, *My son died of Aids: Mandela*, Brand South Africa, 11 Jan 2005.
14. Kevin and Jackie Freiberg, *Madiba Leadership: 5 Lessons Nelson Mandela Taught The World About Change*, Leadership Strategy, July 19, 2018.
15. Freiberg, Madiba Leadership.
16. Koehn, FORGED IN CRISIS.
17. Irin Carmon & Shana Knizhnik, *NOTORIOUS RBG THE LIFE AND TIMES OF RUTH BADER GINSBURG*, 2015, HARPER COLLINS, New York.
18. Carmon & Knizhnik, *NOTORIOUS RBG*.
19. Carmon & Knizhnik, *NOTORIOUS RBG*.
20. Goodwin, *LEADERSHIP IN TURBULENT TIMES*.
21. Goodwin, *LEADERSHIP IN TURBULENT TIMES*.
22. Goodwin, *LEADERSHIP IN TURBULENT TIMES*.
23. www.harriet-tubman.org
24. www.harriet-tubman.org
25. Koehn, FORGED IN CRISIS.
26. Malcolm Muggeridge, *A Man of Conscience*, CBC Television, 1974.
27. Koehn, FORGED IN CRISIS.
28. SHOAH Resource Center. www.yadvashem.org
29. *Biography.com Editors*, The Biography.com website, April 2, 2014.
30. Goodwin, *LEADERSHIP IN TURBULENT TIMES*.

31. Marie Brenner, *The Target*, Vanity Fair, March 15, 2013.
32. *Biography.com Editors*, The Biography.com website, April 2, 2014.
33. Shivani Ekkanath, *10 Facts About Pope Francis' Childhood*, Borgen Magazine, March 31, 2018.
34. Ross Douthat, *Will Pope Francis Break the Church?*, The Atlantic, May 2015.
35. Douthat, *Will Pope Francis Break the Church?*
36. Biography.com Editors, *Pope Francis Biography*, April 12 2018.
37. Biography.com Editors.
38. Biography.com Editors.

3

Leadership in Social Equity, Racism, and Civil Rights

I. Definitions and Background

The Merriam-Webster dictionary defines *racism* as a belief that *race* is the primary *determinant* of human traits and capacities and that racial differences produce an inherent superiority of a particular race.[1] While correct as it stands, this definition falls short in describing the several varieties of racism common in society today. According to RaceForward THE CENTER FOR RACIAL JUSTICE INNOVATION, there are four levels of racism in society today: 1) Internalized, 2) Interpersonal, 3) Institutional, and 4) Structural.[2]

Internalized racism exists within us as individuals and consists of the personal feelings and attitudes each of us have about race. For example, one might consider African Americans not as intelligent or successful as other races simply because they are African American, or one might think Hispanics are prone to crime because they come from countries where drug trading and violence are common. But such internalized racism also exists in individual attitudes about race toward oneself. For example, an African American may hesitate to assert himself or herself among a predominantly white group of people because he or she doesn't feel that they're equal in intelligence or ability, again, because he or she is black. Obviously, these preconceived notions based on race are limiting at best, and harmful to both those experiencing them and those to whom they are directed.

A second level of racism is interpersonal. This level of racism may be the most obvious, in that it is usually the ugliest, most hurtful type exhibited by one American to another. Consider the pain felt by marchers during the Civil Rights marches in the '60s, as they had fire hoses and dogs unleashed on them in Selma, Alabama. Or think of the jeers from baseball fans directed at Jackie Robinson and even Roberto Clemente when they started playing major league baseball. And at a much more apparently innocent level, consider the racist joke that all of us have heard or even told.

While these two levels of racism exist on an individual level, and are most readily apparent, the second two levels probably have a much more harmful *systemic* effect, as they are generally legal and have perhaps a far greater impact on the lives of people of color in the United States.

The first of these is *institutional*, and this form of racism exists in our schools, churches, government offices, and other formally recognized organizations. Consider the substandard, poorly staffed schools in areas where lower socioeconomic groups, usually African American, Hispanic, American Indian, or other similar populations tend to live. Certainly, this is legal but not without the most harmful effects on the lives or these students. Why are the most poorly staffed hospitals located in areas populated by people of color? Probably because the administrators, doctors, nurses, and other medical personnel choose not to work in these same lower socioeconomic areas.

The final systemic level of racism is *structural*. This level encompasses the racism affecting all the institutions of our society. A good example of this is our legal system. Why are African Americans treated differently from whites at all levels—law enforcement, especially in terms of police brutality, prosecution and defense, and in our penal institutions? While open to discussion, few would argue that Michael Brown (Ferguson, Missouri), Trayvon Martin (Sanford, Florida), and Freddie Gray (Baltimore), among other African Americans, were treated differently because of their race.

Another example of structural racism is in our health care system. Why is it that in Louisiana 70.5 percent of the deaths due to the COVID-19 pandemic were African American when they comprise only 32.2 percent of the state's population?[3] Or, in Chicago, why are 69 percent of the COVID-19 deaths among African Americans when they make up only 30 percent of the population?[4] It may be argued that African Americans have more severe underlying conditions such as hypertension or diabetes, but this is only part of the reason. A contributing factor is the availability of adequate health care to African Americans, and for those who have it, reduced quality of care because they are somehow viewed as less deserving because of their race. Figure 3-1 illustrates these four levels of racism.

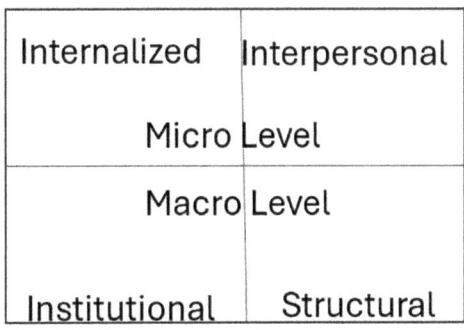

Figure 3-1 Four Levels of Racism. Source: RaceForward Model

While one can identify and describe at least these four levels of racism, it is more difficult to address its causes, and encourage dialogue between whites and people of color, especially African Americans. Part of the reason for this is that racism has been so ingrained in our society, as alluded to in the description of *structural* racism above. Whereas many people, especially whites, see racism as blatantly offensive acts such as those thrust upon African Americans in the 1960s, it is almost common today to see it as "just the way is" (or even should be). Part of the reason for this is that for whites to admit that they are part of a culture that approves of a system in which they are favored because they *are* white, whereas African Americans are less favored, would imply they are *structural* racists, and they cannot do that. Robin DiAngelo describes this thought process in her book *White Fragility*.[5]

Despite the difficulty in talking about the causes of racism, an article in *Psychology Today* offers three human emotions that could lead to racism.[6] The first of these is *fear*. Possibly the most commonly believed reason for which people distrust, or even hate those of another race, is fear. Almost always driven by ignorance, one fears another because he thinks the other person is more violent, stronger physically, or prone to do him harm. The classic example is the white person walking down the street who crosses to the other side when he sees a black person coming toward him.

A second likely motivation for racism is "the need to belong." This motivation is often seen in members of one religious or political sect who distrust, or hate, members of another. Possibly the best modern example of this is that found in the White Supremacist groups that marched on Charlottesville in August of 2017. Their target was the Jewish religion, and as they marched the night before with torches shouting "Jews will not replace us! You will not replace us!" one could not help but sense their ugly sense of solidarity. Behavior which they would not otherwise espouse came very naturally to them marching in a group. Similar behavior was evident in the pre-World War II photographs of crowds of the German people raising their hands and shouting Sieg Heil! toward Hitler as he promised to destroy non-Aryan races. Again, these crowds took comfort in belonging to a group which considered the future of Germany to be in Hitler's hands.

The third element contributing to racism listed in the article is *projection*. Psychologists have long recognized this human tendency to ascribe to others behavior which one subconsciously sees or fears in himself. Perhaps one considers himself of lesser intelligence, but is afraid to admit it, but willingly accuses others (African Americans, Hispanics, Asians) of being less intelligent. Or perhaps one sees in himself an embarrassing desire for wealth at all costs, but, again, being afraid to admit it, will ascribe this greed to others who have been more financially successful. In almost all cases, rather than admit possible shortcomings in himself, the person embracing racist thoughts or ideas finds it is safer and more convenient to accuse others of these same human failures.

II. Extent in U.S. Society

Since the Civil War and the abolition of slavery, the country has come a long way toward reducing racism as marked by events such as Truman desegregating the armed forces in 1948, the Supreme Court declaring racial segregation in schools unconstitutional in 1954, and striking down the state of Virginia's prohibition of interracial marriage in 1967. Yet there have also been events in our nation's history that demonstrate racism is alive and well throughout the country. Examples include law enforcement's use of dogs and firehoses on marching African Americans in Birmingham, Alabama, the attack on John L. Lewis and other marching African Americans on the Edmund Pettus Bridge on Bloody Sunday, March 7, 1965, and, of course, the assassination of Martin Luther King on April 4, 1968, in Memphis. I've already mentioned the Unite the Right march by white supremacists in Charlottesville in 2017.

Such blatant examples of racism have historically been waged against African Americans, but there are other more subtle, generally legal, examples of racism in the United States. Consider these demographic facts.[7]

- Ten richest Americans: 100 percent white

- U.S. Congress: 90 percent white

- U.S. state governors: 96 percent white

- Top military advisors: 100 percent white

- President and vice president: 100 percent white

- U.S. House Freedom Caucus: 100 percent white

- Current U.S. president cabinet: 91 percent white

- People who decide which TV shows we see: 93 percent white

- People who decide which books we read: 90 percent white

- People who decide which news is covered: 85 percent white

- People who decide which music is produced: 95 percent white

- People who directed the one hundred top grossing films of all time: 95 percent white

- Teachers: 82 percent white

- Full-time college professors: 84 percent white

- Owners of men's professional football teams: 97 percent white

These facts clearly suggest that while African Americans are most often affected by racism, it should be recalled that other people of color subject to racism include Hispanics and Asians. The vicious taunts of many for the migrants at our Mexican border is often driven by an almost visceral hatred for Hispanics fleeing several South American countries. The COVID-19 pandemic in the spring of 2020, which began in Wuhan, China, resulted in an increase in verbal attacks on Asians. Clearly, Hispanics, Asians, and other people of color are subject to the same types of racial behavior as African Americans though, perhaps, not to the same degree or vehemence. A study by the Pew Research Center surveyed samplings of white, Asian, Hispanic, and black races, and asked them if they had experienced the following because of their racial identity.[8]

- People acted like they were suspicious of them

- People thought they weren't as smart

- They were treated unfairly in hiring, pay, or promotion

- They were unfairly stopped by police

- They feared for their personal safety

- They were subject to slurs or jokes

- People assumed they were racist or prejudiced

In almost all of these, blacks overwhelmingly responded positively to each of these experiences. For example, 65 percent of blacks experienced people who acted like they were suspicious of them, whereas whites, Asians, and Hispanics experienced much lower percentages of suspicion—25 percent, 34 percent, and 37 percent respectively. Or 44 percent of blacks had been unfairly stopped by police, whereas whites, Asians, and Hispanics reported much lower percentages of police stops—9 percent, 16 percent, and 19 percent respectively.

III. Sustainable Development Impact

Perhaps racism's most glaring affront to sustainable development is it's contradiction of the basic principles upon which our country was founded. This is asserted in many of our founding documents, as, for example, in these immortal words of the Declaration of Independence,

> *We hold these truths to be self-evident, that* all men are created equal, *that they are endowed by their Creator with certain unalienable Rights, that among these are Life, Liberty, and the Pursuit of Happiness.*

Abraham Lincoln refers specifically to the promise of our founding fathers in this Gettysburg Address,

Four score and seven years ago our fathers brought forth on this continent, a new nation, conceived in Liberty, and dedicated to the proposition that all men are created equal.

And even more defining of the rights of all citizens, regardless of "race, color, or previous conditions of servitude," are Articles XIV and XV of the Constitution which guarantee due process and other rights to all.

Another reason racism impedes sustainable development is its effect on diversity or lack thereof. Most people are familiar with the concept in nature that diversity of plant and animal life promotes species growth and evolution. Regarding plant life, if there are a number of different crops on a piece of land, their diversity is conducive to their survival. If some are susceptible to a given pest, or have a greater need for rainfall or irrigation, those that are not susceptible will more likely survive and grow.

A similar situation occurs with people. Among different races, it is likely that members will have different predispositions, skills, abilities, and likes and dislikes. This doesn't imply that members of one race are better than another, but only that they respond to different challenges differently. Thus, in society, or in the workplace, a greater variety of participants (races) responding to a variety of different needs is conducive to healthy growth. And one of the results of this is growth of those populations which adapt most readily to environmental and other challenges.

Related to this is the growth in absolute numbers of the world's and national populations. Much of the developed world is experiencing slower population growth and this, in turn, is making it more difficult for their economies to grow. One example is Japan where the population growth rate for the last ten years has actually been negative. In the U.S., however, there has been growth in population in the same period, although still at a growth rate of less than 1 percent.⁹

Part of the reason for at least this minimal growth has been the increased proportion of African American, Latino, and Asian population, especially Latino. Whereas the population of whites in the U.S., was 59.5 percent in 2020, it is projected to decline to 55.3 percent in 2030, 51.2 percent in 2040, and 47.2 percent in 2050, but the percentage of Latinos in 2020 was 19.0 percent and increased to 21.5 percent in 2030, 24.1 percent in 2040, and 26.5 percent in 2050. Clearly, the loss in population percentages by whites, was more than compensated by the increased percentage of Latinos, resulting in an overall increase in population.[10]

This growth is positive for the U.S., but there is still the issue of health as an integral part of sustainable development. For many reasons, throughout the world and the United States, there are disparities between both the availability of health care and the degree of good health among people of color compared to whites. There is a greater occurrence of high blood pressure among blacks in the United Kingdom than whites. The infant mortality rate for children younger than 12 months is 62.3 per 1,000 for people of color in Brazil as opposed to 37.3 per 1,000 among whites. The life expectancy is 56.9 and 61.7 years for Indigenous men and women in Australia, as opposed to 75.2 and 81.1 years for non-indigenous men and women. In the U.S., the death rate from diabetes is 27.8 per 1,000 black people, whereas it is only 7.3 per 1,000 whites.[11] Clearly, these differences for people of color are not sustainable for their contribution to the overall health of any nation, especially given their disproportionate share in the growth of many nations today.

In addition to these more humanitarian aspects of race with respect to sustainable development, there are the economic or financial considerations.[12] For example, the average household wealth of black families in the United States is $17,000, only one tenth that of white households. Or it's an established fact that black-owned firms find it much more difficult to access credit than white-owned firms. And another related example of the effect of racism on the economy is the fact that black unemployment is consistently much higher than white.

Such statistics argue, at least from a sustainable development viewpoint, for a much more inclusive attitude toward people of color—especially African Americans—in the nation's economic system. This is especially true considering the historical treatment of black Americans in the United States. But aside from this humanitarian viewpoint, there is evidence that racial diversity is good for business also. According to a McKinsey Report[13] companies in the top quartile for racial diversity are 35 percent more likely to enjoy better financial returns than similar companies in their industry. And for every ten percent increase in racial and ethnic diversity, earnings before interest and taxes (EBIT) increases by 0.8 percent.

IV. Leadership Opportunities

A. Government

Probably the most obvious way someone in government can display leadership in decreasing racism in both government and society is through public declamation. Leaders in government have daily opportunities to say why racism is wrong, and such opportunities set the tone for everything his or her branch of government does.

Depending on the form of government, such leaders can influence legislation targeting racism and setting in place policies that make outward displays of racism a crime. Consider legislation which deems certain crimes "hate crimes," especially at the federal level. Congress has done this, in which case such legislation becomes the "law of the land," and makes it more unlikely that crimes against African Americans, other people of color, or persons of alternative sexual preference will occur. Similar opportunities for leadership at state and local levels exist for governors, state legislators, and mayors for issues over which they have control, such as ensuring voting rights for African Americans.

Leaders can affect the decrease (or growth) of racism in their choice of administrators who set policy affecting immigrants and people of color. Consider the influence of the Department of Homeland Security in determining which races will achieve admission to this country. Or consider the Department of Justice in its efforts to address protests of African Americans seeking protection from police violence. In all these cases the degree to which racism is not only prevented but, in fact, redressed, is a function of the racial attitudes of the leaders responsible for enforcing anti-discrimination or hate crime laws.

B. Business, Organizations or Industry

While not as effective as government leaders, leaders in business, industry, or other organizations bear a similar responsibility in addressing and reducing racism in their organizations. Consider the effort by Starbucks in forming its Starbucks Black Partner Network and support of Black Lives Matter during the summer of 2020.[14] Such efforts are not only good for business but ensure a long lasting relationship with its customers of all races.

The leaders of religious organizations, nonprofits, and Non-Governmental Organizations (NGOs) have a special responsibility to exercise leadership in issues of race. By virtue of their commitment to a higher ideal, their efforts to reduce or eliminate racism in not only their organization, but in society as well, present a more convincing message for racial equality.

Also, leaders in certain industries, businesses, and entertainment have a special responsibility to use their notoriety to deliver a stronger message on racism. Recently, Mike Krzyzewski, the Duke University basketball coach, presented his thoughts on Black Lives Matter in a short, but very powerful video.[15] His words are more convincing, not only because of his success as a winning basketball coach who has coached many young African Americans, but as a West Point graduate who refers back to lessons he was taught about "doing the right thing." Numerous other examples of similar opportunities in the sports and entertainment worlds come to mind.

C. Individuals

There are opportunities for individuals to show leadership in the face of racism in everyday life. In the event someone tells a joke disparaging or making fun of someone of color, the proper thing to do would be to remind the person telling the joke that you don't think the joke is appropriate, or at the very least, to withhold comment or not laugh at the joke.

Almost daily there are articles in the local newspaper concerning some issue of civil rights or racism nationally or in the community. An excellent way to display individual leadership would be to send a letter to the editor commenting on the issue and showing support for racial equality or some other aspect of civil rights. By including one's name on the letter the originator makes public his or her position on the issue and invites comment by other readers. In so doing the content of the original newspaper issue on racism or civil rights is perhaps extended to an exchange of ideas within the community, and perhaps leads toward the advance of more understanding of the issue.

There were numerous marches throughout the country protesting police brutality against African Americans in the summer of 2020. While many participants were African American, there were also many white Americans marching in support of their black fellow citizens. This in itself was an act of leadership resulting in the decision of many other white Americans to join in the peaceful protest. Similarly, many white households displayed "Peace and Justice" yard signs on their property showing solidarity with African Americans. Again, this open display of support was an influence on other neighbors to support racial equality.

V. Examples of Leadership in Social Equity

Probably the best way to illustrate leadership in social equity is to show actual examples of leadership in which men and women have distinguished themselves in a particular area—in this case, racial concern. A helpful way to do this is to consider the same three broad areas in which such leadership has been evident: government or the military, business or institutional, and individual. Government, the area most usually considered when one thinks of leadership, and the individual are reasonably well defined. But the second area, business or institutional, is broader in scope and can include professional sports figures, entertainers, or those in the business world. The one characteristic of the men and women who have so distinguished themselves in displaying their belief in the fair and equal treatment of all human beings, regardless of race, is profound leadership. Examples of these follow.

A. Government

Lyndon B. Johnson

Lyndon B. Johnson, the thirty-sixth president of the United States, is probably best known for two things: 1) he succeeded the assassinated John F. Kennedy as president; and 2) he was the president during the years in which the country began and was deepening its long involvement in Vietnam. What he is generally not known for, however, is his fierce advocacy for the civil rights of African Americans. However, this should not be such a surprise, when his skills as a senator were influential in passing the Civil Rights Act of 1957.

Shortly after assuming office in 1963 LBJ gathered his closest advisors and laid out the goals for civil rights[16] in his new administration: 1) he would see that Kennedy's planned civil rights act would be passed; 2) he would ensure that everyone had the right to vote (obviously referring to African Americans, given the state of race relations in the country at the time); and 3) he would see to it that everyone had a right to education, again, referring to the state of civil rights in the nation, but also, perhaps, a reflection of his early years as a teacher in his native Texas. These goals would be at the forefront of his agenda when he wasn't trying to solve the Vietnam dilemma, and they were central to the overriding goal of his Great Society, which was racial and economic justice.

As president, Johnson devoted all his energy and relationships from his days in the Senate to securing true equality for African Americans. While he had always believed in the need for racial equality, certainly since working as a senator on the 1957 Civil Rights Act, he was in a position now to correct the racial injustice he saw in the country. Part of this sensitivity to the state of racial inequality arose from personal experiences. For some time, he would typically have his butler and housemaid, Gene and Helen Williams, and his cook Zepher Wright—all African Americans—drive his personal car back and forth to Texas at the change of congressional sessions. Then one day the butler mentioned how exhausting the drive back to Texas was getting since they were unable to find a place to stay during the trip that would allow 'colored' people to stay or at least use restroom facilities. And on another occasion Johnson remarked to the leader of the Congress of Racial Equality that Wright—a college graduate—had to go out into a field to relieve himself on these trips. Seeing these instances of racial injustice still common throughout the nation—especially the south—only fueled Johnson's personal feelings about the way African Americans were still treated in the twentieth century, and his desire to do something about it. So he was determined to use all of his negotiating skills acquired in his years in the Senate to right what he perceived as a serious wrong in the United States—the extreme mistreatment of African Americans.

At the same time LBJ took a considerable risk in alienating and losing the support of his own party in the south. Nonetheless, he undertook an effort to pass a much-needed civil rights act without the shortcomings of the Civil Rights Act of 1957. The first step was to have the proposed bill moved out of the committee led by an opponent of the bill in the House of Representatives using an obscure provision called a discharge petition. Under this provision a stalled bill could be sent to the full house with the vote of more than half its members (at least 218). After lobbying numerous members of the House through many conversations, which he questionably recorded, he was able to get the proposed civil rights act out of committee. The House then passed the bill which then went on to the Senate.

Here, opposition to the proposed civil rights act was even more severe, led by staunch states' rights senators from the south. It's important to note that the very cultural tradition of the south was at stake, a tradition of which even Johnson was a part, except, that is, for his fierce determination to achieve equality for African Americans. The fight was on, and even though his party (Democratic) held the majority, those opposed to the proposed civil rights bill vowed to hold what was to become the longest filibuster in history, which could only be stopped with a super majority of 67 votes. Finally, after 75 days and 500 hours of filibuster, only one more vote was needed to break the filibuster and attain the requisite 67 votes. That one vote happened to lie with Senator Clair Engle of California, who was currently away suffering from a brain tumor. But Johnson was able to use his considerable influence to have the stricken senator flown in and brought to the Senate in a wheelchair to cast the deciding vote to break the filibuster. After that, it was a relatively easy matter to pass into law the Civil Rights Act of 1964.

The Civil Rights Act of 1964 was sweeping in the changes it brought to government and society in the country.[17] Of possibly the greatest significance was the fact that it ended segregation in all public places. No longer could there be drinking fountains labeled "Whites" or "Colored." It prohibited discrimination based on race, gender, or religion by employers and labor unions, and to enforce this prohibition, it created the Equal Employment Opportunity Commission. It also prohibited the use of federal money in activities practicing discrimination. And to ensure desegregation in public schools, it gave the Department of Education (then Office of Education) the power to enforce it. Finally, it barred the unequal application of voting requirements, which, in turn, led to the Voting Rights Act of 1965.

While the initial steps toward passing the Civil Rights Act of 1964 were taken by John F. Kennedy, probably no other person showed more leadership in having it passed in its final form than Lyndon B. Johnson.

B. Organizations, Business, and Institutions

Branch Rickey

Branch Rickey was born December 20, 1881, in Scioto County, Ohio, to a Methodist farming family. With this background he grew up with strong religious values, which probably influenced his personal and business decisions in later life.[18] But early on, he displayed considerable athletic talent, especially in baseball and football, and even made it to what were then the professional leagues in both sports. He also had a natural skill for managing other athletes, coaching football, baseball, and basketball while he was the Athletic Director at Ohio Wesleyan, which he had attended as an undergraduate.

Among the first exposures to racism for Rickey occurred when he was a student athlete baseball coach at Ohio Wesleyan University in 1904.[19] On one road trip, a black player on the team was prohibited from staying at a hotel because of his race. Rickey objected to this, saying that the whole team stays, or not at all, whereupon he set up a cot in his room for the black player, so the team could stay together. Another formative experience early in life was his friendship with Charles W. Follis, a black teammate while they were both playing professional football for the Shelby

A.A. team.[20] Follis was under a great deal of pressure from being the only African American on the team, but always handled it well, and was able to excel both as a player and a person. This did not escape the attention of Rickey, and it is felt that his admiration for Follis influenced his decision later in life to seek out and sign African Americans to play in Major League Baseball.

The first of these, of course, was Jackie Robinson, the first African American to play on a Major League Baseball team. In 1945, Rickey, as General Manager of the Brooklyn Dodgers, would seek out talented African Americans to play in the major leagues because he thought it a good thing for society. And Jackie Robinson was not only an African America, but an excellent ball player. Rickey signed him in 1947, and he became the first African American to play on a major league baseball team, and he was voted the American League rookie of the year.

After this momentous event—for both major league baseball and American society—Rickey went on to sign Roy Campanella and Don Newcombe for the Dodgers, two more African Americans, who helped the Dodgers win pennants in 1949, 1952, 1953, 1955, and 1956.[21]

Throughout his life Branch Rickey displayed a quality of leadership, as a player, coach, and successful baseball executive who recognized the dignity and worth of African Americans in both sports and life. Arguably, no other person was as responsible as he for integrating African Americans into professional sports, and by extension, American society.

C. Individual Leadership Example

Rosa Parks

Rosa Parks was born Rosa Louise McCauley on February 4, 1913 in Tuskegee, Alabama. At a very early age she went with her mother to live in a small town with her grandparents. Both her grandparents had been slaves, and in their new life of freedom they maintained a strong sense of racial equality. It was said that her grandfather would stand in front of their house with a shotgun as the Ku Klux Klan in menacing head coverings marched by their house. And Rosa showed the same internal defiance as she watched her grandparents. In one instance, as she was being bullied by an older white boy, she stood by with a rock in her hand until her grandmother cautioned her not to use it. Rosa's reply then foretold an inner defiance as she replied, "I would rather be lynched than live to be mistreated and not be allowed to say, 'I don't like it.'"[22]

School segregation was common, and the white students were able to take a bus to a new school building, while the black children had to walk some distance to attend their dilapidated schoolhouse.

When she was eleven, she attended the Industrial School for Girls, which proved to be a defining experience for her. Alice L. White, a white woman from Boston, founded and operated the school, and she had a tremendous influence on Rosa. For one thing she showed Rosa that not all white people were bad. And for another, she and the school instilled in Rosa a sense of self-respect and the belief that she could do something significant with her life.[23] Rosa then attended Alabama State Teachers College, but had to leave in the 11th grade to care for her mother and grandmother.

When she was eighteen and doing domestic work, a white friend of her employer tried to sexually assault her, assuming it was his right to do so, explaining that her employer permitted it. Rosa resisted and explained later in her private papers that she was determined to die before consenting to the white friend of her employer.

In 1932, when she was nineteen, Rosa married Raymond Parks, a member of the NAACP. As she worked as a seamstress, she continued her strong interest in civil rights conditioned by her experiences in childhood, and her observations of the racial inequality of the time. Eventually, she joined the Montgomery NAACP in 1943 and became a youth leader, as well as the secretary to the chapter president.

During this period of "Jim Crow" laws she joined her activist husband in opposing the many legal tactics used to segregate African Americans from the many civic and educational opportunities enjoyed by whites. Raymond Parks had earlier been active in defending the Scottsboro Boys, nine African Americans who were unjustly accused of raping two white women. Rosa was active in raising money for their defense. She also led an effort in 1944 to prosecute several white men who raped a young black woman at gunpoint.[24]

But while she was active as a young woman opposing the many instances of segregation at the time and protecting black women from sexual assault by white men, Rosa Parks is best known for one incident in December of 1955. She was on her way home from work on one of the public busses on which African Americans and whites were assigned separate seating. As passengers got on the bus at one of its stops, it ran out of seats in the white section, at which point the bus driver asked her to give up her seat to one of the white passengers without a seat. She refused, and the bus driver had the police arrest her. The Montgomery Improvement Association, which had recently appointed Martin Luther King, Jr. as its president, knowing that African Americans constituted by far the greatest portion of ridership on the city buses, decided to stage a boycott in the black community.

The boycott lasted 382 days and was a huge success. The boycott drew attention to the inequity of separate seating on buses and other segregation practices in public places—the so-called Jim Crow laws. As a result, a local district court declared such practices illegal, which was upheld by the Supreme Court and led to one of the most significant victories against racial segregation up to that point.

Even though Rosa Parks had served tirelessly throughout her twenties in her fight for racial equality, her refusal to give up her seat on a bus that December in 1955 was special. Along with the Supreme Court's decision in *Brown v. Board of Education* in 1954, it marked the beginning of the tumultuous string of events in the peaceful fight for racial equality in the '60s in the United States.

Unfortunately for Parks, she and her husband were the victims of death threats and job losses due to the boycott, and they moved to Detroit in 1957. There they both continued to fight for racial and social justice, Parks becoming the secretary to U.S. Representative John Conyers of Michigan, himself a fierce advocate for racial equality.

Even though she is best known for her courageous refusal to give up her seat to a white man on a bus, which led to the Montgomery bus boycott, Rosa Parks accomplished much more than that. During the years leading up to the boycott, and afterward in Detroit, she was a staunch defender of those African Americans who were denied civil rights or unjustly accused of crimes, many examples of which were only revealed in her later writings. In 1979 she was honored by the NAACP with its most prestigious award, the Spingarn Medal. At the time, she was only the sixty-fourth person to have been so honored. In

1996 President Bill Clinton awarded her the Presidential Medal of Freedom, and in 1997 she received the Congressional Gold Medal, which is the highest award given by Congress. Two years later *TIME* magazine recognized her many accomplishments in her lifelong fight for racial equality by naming her one of "The 20 Most Influential People of the 20th Century."

These awards and acts of recognition are especially apropos for Rosa Parks. For, without them, many of her accomplishments, except for the Montgomery boycott, would go unnoticed. But, because of them, and the description of the many activities in her life which warranted them, we now recognize Rosa Parks as one of the most influential leaders in the struggle for racial equality and civil rights in our lifetime.

References

1. 2020 Merriam-Webster, Incorporated.
2. *Moving the Race Conversation Forward*, RaceForward | 2014
3. Deborah Barfield Berry, *Black people are overwhelmingly dying from coronavirus in cities across the US*, USA Today, April 7, 2020.
4. Cheyenne Haslett, *CDC releases new data as debate grows over racial disparities in coronavirus deaths*, abcNEWS, April 8, 2020.
5. Robin Diangelo, *White Fragility, Why It's So Hard for White People to Talk About Racism*, Beacon Press, 2018.
6. Allison Abrams, LCSW-R, *The Psychology Behind Racism*, Psychology Today, Sept. 6, 2017.
7. Diangelo, *White Fragility*.
8. Juliana Menasce Horowitz, Anna Brown and Kiana Cox, *Race in America 2019*, Pew Research Center, April 2019.
9. Worldometer.
10. 2020 The National Equity Atlas.

11. Vernellia R. Randall, *Racism Health and Sustainable Development*, Institute on Race, Health Care and the Law, March 10, 2010.
12. Eshe Nelson, *The dismal cost of economics' lack of racial diversity*, Quartz, Dec. 16, 2018.
13. Vivian Hunt, Dennis Layton, and Sara Prince, *Why Diversity Matters*, McKinsey & Company, January 2015.
14. Roz, Rossann and Zing, *Standing together against racial injustice*, June 12, 2020, Starbucks Stories & News.
15. Ellen J. Horrow, *Duke basketball coach Mike Krzyzewski speaks out in powerful Black Lives Matter video*, USA Today, June 26, 2020.
16. Nancy Koehn, FORGED IN CRISIS THE POWER OF COURAGEOUS LEADERSHIP IN TURBULENT TIMES, Scribners, 2017.
17. www.history.com
18. Andy McCue, *Branch Rickey*, SOCIETY FOR AMERICAN BASEBALL RESEARCH (University of Nebraska Press, 2012).
19. David Oshinsky, *The Man Who Hired Jackie Robinson*, NYTimes, March 25, 2011.
20. Kimberly Nash, *Breaking Pro Football's Color Line: The Story of Charles W. Follis*, Bleacher Report.
21. Steven Marcus, *Jackie Robinson and Branch Rickey: Together in History*, Newsday, February 25, 2017.
22. Jeanne Theoharis, *How history got the Rosa Parks story wrong*, Washington Post, Dec. 1, 2015.
23. David Harmon, *Montgomery Industrial School for Girls*, Encyclopedia of Alabama, May 4, 2007.
24. Shira Tarlo, *Rosa Parks Birthday: 5 Things You May Not Know About Civil Rights Icon*, NBC NEWS, Feb. 4, 2017.

4

Leadership in Social Equity— Homelessness

I. Definitions and Background

A. Definitions

A basic definition of being homeless, according to the Meriam Webster Dictionary is "not having a home or permanent place of residence." But this simplifies the term, and the Department of Housing and Urban Development (HUD) goes a bit further and states, "Any person living in a temporary location, such as a shelter or a place not fit for human habitation (encampment, car, abandoned building, etc.) is considered homeless." And even this is generally insufficient given the many federal and other programs which depend on a much more detailed description of homelessness. Here again, HUD, as of January 4, 2012, provides four distinct characterizations of homelessness.[1]

The first of these is a condition in which people live in circumstances not generally considered fit for human habitation or a shelter. This, of course, covers all those situations which people generally think of when they consider homelessness, such as under bridges, bypasses, or other places which provide some shelter from the environment. While this is the type of homelessness which people think of when they hear the term, there are other aspects of it which lead to a person's becoming homeless or affect his or her ability to avoid it.

Another type of homelessness is the situation in which a person did have a place to live, even if it's just a hotel or motel room, but is in danger of losing that within fourteen days without an apparent alternative. The person may not be homeless now, but for all intents and purposes, is still considered homeless since he or she knows there will be no place to live in the near future.

And yet another type of homeless family is one with children up to twenty-four years of age and which is "unstably housed." Unstably housed is a condition characterized by one of the following: 1) the family has not owned or leased its housing for at least sixty days and does not have a reasonable expectation to continue doing so beyond that period; 2) it has made two or more moves in the last sixty days; or 3) is unlikely to leave its current housing because of disability or unemployment. The implication here is that the family has no reasonable certainty that it will continue living in the current housing for the foreseeable future and is thus unable to make what would otherwise be considered normal life decisions, such as providing potential employers a home address.

A fourth condition of homelessness is one in which the person has fled domestic violence, sexual assault, or other dangerous conditions without assurance of another place to live.

B. Causes

Just as there are several definitions of homelessness, there are five commonly accepted causes: 1) Housing (or lack thereof); 2) Income; 3) Health; 4) Domestic Violence; and 5) Racial Inequality.[2]

Possibly at the top of this list is a nationwide shortage of affordable housing. As the economy grew after the Second World War, decent wage paying jobs were plentiful, and housing construction increased to meet the demand of those who could afford it. However, beginning in the 1970s, and into the 1980s, wages stagnated, and the supply of affordable houses dwindled to the point where currently eight million low-income people have to spend at least half their income on housing.[2]

Of course, the other side of the equation is low income. In many cases there are specific reasons for which those seeking housing fail to find it, such as lack of education, criminal history, unavoidable gaps in work history, or an unfavorable labor market. But overall, for whatever reason, wages have not increased appreciably over the last thirty years.

A particularly unfortunate cause of homelessness is physical or mental disability, and, ironically, the condition of homelessness often causes or exacerbates illnesses, such tuberculosis, Hepatitis C, or other diseases caused by filth or infestation. It's a fact, according to the Department of Housing and Urban Development, that homeless persons are twice as likely to have physical or mental impairment compared to those housed. And, in 2017, 20 percent of the homeless were found to have a mental disability. What's more, 16 percent of those homeless experienced some type of substance abuse, and at least 10,000 homeless suffered from HIV/AIDS. As a result, the incidence of serious diseases such as heart disease and diabetes was found to be between three and six times as common in the homeless. It's no surprise then, that at least 10 percent of those seeking care for substance abuse or mental illness in the public health system are homeless.[2]

A particularly tragic cause of homelessness, because it is so infrequently discussed, is domestic violence. Whether married or not, one of the partners—usually the woman— suffers physical or mental abuse at the hands of the other. Other factors such as financial or emotional dependence keep them together until the domestic violence becomes unbearable, and one of them—again, usually the woman—must leave the only home she has known. On a given night in 2019, 48,000 beds in shelters were set aside for victims of domestic violence.[2] In addition to the other adverse effects of homelessness such as the loss of personal dignity, emotional distress, and the deprivation of basic living comforts, personal safely is of paramount importance in the domestic violence cause of homelessness.

Racial inequality is as prevalent in homelessness as it is in other issues of social equity. While it exists disproportionately in many different races, it is particularly destructive to the African American community. Even though African Americans make up only 13 percent of the America population, they constitute 40 percent of its homeless population. And there are many reasons for this stemming from other issues of social inequity such as poverty, discrimination in rental housing, and incarceration. Since 27.4 percent of African Americans live in poverty, it's no wonder that they make up such a large proportion of homeless. It's an accepted fact, supported by research conducted by the Department of Housing and Urban Development, that African Americans are more often steered away from affordable housing than other races. Given that the incarceration rate of African Americans between 1968 and 2016 was at least six times that of white Americans, it's no wonder that access to available housing was limited where questions on prior incarceration was a qualifying issue.[2]

II. Extent in U.S. Society

The officially recognized count of the homeless population in the United States is that provided by the U.S. Census Bureau taken every four years. The two main categories of homeless are those from Service-Based Enumeration (SBE) and Enumeration at Transitory Locations (ETL).[3] As the name implies, SBE includes services such as shelters with sleeping facilities, shelters for children who've run away or been subject to neglect, soup kitchens and other facilities offering food, and targeted outdoor locations such as campgrounds. Obviously, this differentiation facilitates identifying and enumerating homeless populations. According to the 2010 Census, the total number of homeless people in the U.S. was 422,972, which was a 49 percent increase over the 2000 Census.[3]

The second category of homeless was that provided by Enumeration at Transitory Locations, which includes sites such as college dorms, hotels and motels, and other such temporary locations. In 2019 the total homeless population in the U.S. was 567,715. Of these, 396,045 were individuals, and 171,670 were members of families. Among the individuals, approximately half the population were sheltered, whereas most families lived in sheltered conditions. The breakdown by race and ethnicity is especially telling. Of particular significance is the disproportionate number of people of color in the homeless population. Especially among African Americans, the number of their homeless is almost equal to the white total even though their proportion of the total population is much less. The same is true, albeit to a lesser extent, for Hispanics.[4]

Another differentiating characteristic of homelessness, especially as it relates to sustainable development, is whether or not the homeless population is living in a sheltered or unsheltered condition. Whereas 37 percent of the total homeless (including individuals and families) live in unsheltered conditions, the percentage jumps to 50 percent among individuals.[4] Possibly the most striking example of the pain of homelessness is living without shelter in January or February in a city like Chicago, New York City, or Boston.

Other factors which increase the pain of homelessness include the age and physical condition of the homeless, as well as external factors which only make a bad situation worse. Certainly, the age of those experiencing homelessness is a contributing factor, this because older persons are more susceptible to physical ailments which exacerbate the harsh conditions of just living day-to-day. And then there are unexpected occurrences which either cause additional homelessness or accentuate the suffering of the currently homeless. At this writing there are an historically record number of fires in the western states of the country, especially California, and more frequent than usual hurricanes affecting the Gulf States. All these events either cause thousands to be homeless that weren't before, or simply add to the misery of those already homeless.

Also, at this writing the nation (and world) is in the middle of the COVID-19 pandemic. As terrible as this infection is, it doubly affects those who are homeless. How does one quarantine or otherwise socially isolate when testing positive for this virus when there is no home? At the same time, it's been shown that the homeless population is much more likely to contract the disease due to the conditions under which they may be living, such as in crowded shelters, or "doubling up" with friends or relatives, or just sharing the minimal comfort of a fire or wind break.

Regardless of the specific circumstances and causes of homelessness, it is enlightening to consider its personal impact on human beings. The most obvious, of course, is the loss of protection from the elements in the form of rain, heat, cold, and snow. And, related to this is the loss of personal security and protection of one's belongings, things which most of us probably take for granted in our homes or apartments.

Possibly of greatest significance is the loss of personal dignity in losing or having lost one's home. One cannot help but feel a sense of shame in not being able to provide shelter for his or her children or even herself. And there are other related consequences as well. In the book, *Evicted*, the point is made that "Residential stability begets a kind of psychological stability."[5] This, in turn, makes it difficult for the individual or members of a family to develop the strong social connections which are conducive to healthy living.

It is natural to ask what is the trend of homelessness in the U.S. For greater insight it helps to consider only the 11.8 percent of the U.S. population that lives in poverty, as they are at the greatest risk of becoming homeless. Among these, there are those who spend at least 50 percent of their income on housing. In 2018 the number of homeless in this group was 6.5 million, but this also includes almost 4 million who were living "doubled up," or in a multifamily situation.[6] In other words, this latter group was at greater risk of becoming homeless due to the possibility of broken families or friendships.

While the growth in people at risk for homelessness has declined somewhat between 2014 and 2018, the number of both the total and those living "doubled up" has increased over 1 percent a year since 2007. And since the majority of at-risk population consists of those living "doubled up," the precariousness of being at risk for homelessness is even more than its poverty condition alone would suggest.

The significance of these homeless numbers is most evident when compared with the numbers in other developed countries. And even then, the definitions of homelessness and means of gathering data vary by country. This notwithstanding, the Organization for Economic Co-operation and Development (OECD) has compiled such data and compares the degree of homelessness for several major developed nations.

Regarding the numbers of homeless per 100,000 in population for these nations, France fares worst at 217, followed by the United

States at 177, and several others.[7] These include Ireland, Spain, and Portugal, with 78, 49, and 20. Clearly, and for many reasons, there is a wide disparity among nations with regard to homelessness.

The reasons for these disparities are probably many, but most likely include the types of government, ranging from strictly capitalist to socialist, but also other difficult to define characteristics such as social conscience. In any case, the fact that there is a discernible degree of homelessness in such developed countries indicates a need for attention toward solving this drag on sustainable economic development in even the most advanced nations.

III. Sustainable Development Impact

A. Impact on the Individual

The impact of homelessness on sustainability can be viewed in two ways: the impact on the individual or family themselves and the impact of homelessness on society. The impact on the individual is most strongly felt by considering the things which having a home—or any place to live—provides. Probably the most obvious of these is health. By having protection from the elements, such as a roof over one's head and walls to keep out the wind, a person stands a better chance of staying healthy. In the worldwide COVID-19 pandemic of 2020, having a consistent form of shelter enabled an individual to avoid contagion by remaining apart from carriers of disease. Just having a place to rest regularly is conducive to both mental and physical health.

Having a home, apartment, or other place to stay reliably provides personal safety. Having a place to guard one's personal safely and one's personal possessions allows one to ensure a sustainable future, one which a person can count on, knowing that it is likely that these physical things will be there.

Regarding the essence of sustainability, having a home or other place to live with assurance that it will be there tomorrow provides the means and place to satisfy life's basic needs, and satisfying these basic needs means that a person will continue to thrive into the future. Reliable housing affords access to the simple things, such as doing the laundry, having a place to prepare and eat food, perhaps invite others to share hospitality, all of which provide the essence of growing as a human being.

Regarding the sustainable impact on the person, there is the feeling of security, or belongingness that only a home or place to reliably stay can provide. Even the simplest domicile in the form of a tent can provide the feeling of belonging. It may be a modest apartment or room in a boarding house that one calls home, but the simplest abode can provide the emotional security that is lacking without it. With reliable housing a person can plan for a future that was unimaginable when he or she was homeless.

B. Impact on Society

There are numerous impacts on society from homelessness in a given area. While the socioeconomic (financial) impacts are especially acute in a large metropolitan area such as Los Angeles, Chicago, or New York, the documented impact on a smaller city such as Olympia, Washington, is especially telling.[8] In 2015 there were 476 documented homeless individuals in this city, although the actual number was probably closer to 700. But even with this relatively small population in a city of 54,427 in 2020, the homeless population accounted for some $130 million of municipal expenditures due mostly to medical costs and incarceration expenses, which is about $186,000 per homeless person. This financial drain on the city is even more significant when one considers that these homeless individuals are not contributing to the economic development of the city.

Conversely, the existence of homeless individuals sleeping in doorways, abandoned buildings, and on public walkways and transportation interferes with the commercial development of the city. Business owners find themselves in the difficult circumstance of having to show empathy for those less fortunate than themselves while they struggle to provide for their own families by operating a small business.

Undeniably the outward appearance of homelessness distracts from home values in a given area. Those looking to purchase a home cannot help but wonder what are the circumstances in that area which have led to so many people in the community being homeless. Those who do settle in the area discount the price they are willing to pay for a home because of the outward appearance of the area. The result is an overall reduction in home values, which detracts from sustainable development in the area.

Another impact of homelessness is experienced by areas that depend heavily on tourism. Unfortunately, the same geographical features which make an area a nice place to visit, such as mild weather and access to public services, make that area one in which a person can remain homeless. The result is that fewer tourists choose to visit with the loss of income to all residents and diminished sustainable development.

A very real physical impact of homelessness is the environmental damage that often results from people livening in makeshift encampments, under highway overpasses, and other places which provide minimal shelter. Without systems of trash pickup generally provided to homes and apartment buildings, discarded food waste and litter are left to decay in place, attracting scavenging animals and insects. Encampments near streams, rivers, and waterways pose a significant danger to water quality from water runoff from these areas. Ultimately, the water supply of the entire area becomes unsustainable for businesses and homes.

Unfortunately, the same conditions which lead to the increase in homelessness in a given area also lead to higher than average drug use by those seeking some escape from their living conditions. This, in turn, leads to discarded drug paraphernalia such as needles which pose a danger to wildlife and children in the area. Again, the buildup of harmful items is not conducive to sustainable development.

Perhaps the most significant impact on sustainable development by homelessness is on the physical health of the community in which it exists. The spread of contagious disease is rampant due to the unsanitary living conditions of most homeless encampments. In 2017 an outbreak of hepatitis A in San Diego tied to homeless encampments was responsible for the spread of the disease to 500 persons in California, and the deaths of 19 persons in San Diego.[9] The epidemic caused a renewed interest in homelessness, especially in San Diego, where it increased 14 percent in 2017, and prompted statewide efforts to address housing shortages in California.

IV. Leadership Opportunities to Address Homelessness

A. Government

The problem of homelessness is so pervasive that only an overseeing body, such as the state and local government, can address it with any degree of success. At the same time, it is important to realize that there are vast regional differences throughout the country which relegate the issue of homelessness to state government responsibility. Within individual states there is a clear divergence of responsibility (and resources) between state and local government. At the state level, there is much greater access to resources, given its taxing authority, primarily income taxes, and its access to federal grants and revenue sharing. Also, state government is much more able to comprehend the "big picture" of homelessness throughout its state. Consequently, states develop policies and programs that best address the challenge of homelessness.

It should also be recognized that local and municipal governments are better able to implement these policies and programs for their citizens. First, local governments are much more aware of the requirements and needs of the homeless population in their jurisdictions. What's more, being closer to actual conditions of homelessness, local governments are much more suited to evaluate the success of the programs developed by the state government. Finally, local governments have a stake in these programs and will do whatever it takes to ensure their success.

California is a good example of the approach taken by government to address homelessness, not only because of the proportion of its peoples' income spent on housing, up to 60 percent of income for the lowest quartile of population,[10] but also because nearly half of the homeless population of the U.S. live in that state.[11] The cost of housing has only made the problem worse and makes it more difficult to find solutions. As noted, the role of government, in this case California's state government, is primarily in developing policies and programs that can be applied throughout the state.[12]

Among these are programs that support building new affordably priced housing. These programs often provide favorable regulatory treatment for those developers who commit to reserving a portion of new housing construction for low-income housing. Or they may provide incentives to adjust zoning restrictions to enable the construction of such housing.

Another category is programs that help households afford housing. Again, there are many ways to do this, including the subsidy of rental or ownership costs, possible adjustment of property taxes, or incentives to make home ownership more attractive to those who couldn't otherwise afford it.

Finally, there are Health and Human Services programs that may assist with preventing homelessness. These programs may not directly deal with the issue of homelessness, but rather address other issues, such as mental illness or drug addiction, which lead to homelessness.

Cities and counties are generally better prepared to implement these programs at the local level, and a good example is the city of San Diego.[13] The local responsible governing body is the San Diego Homeless Commission, and it oversees several programs recognized and supported by the city. Among these is Operation Shelter to Home in the San Diego Convention Center & Golden Hall. As the name suggests, this program made use of otherwise vacant spaces during the COVID-19 pandemic of 2020. These facilities were especially suited for this purpose at that time, given their enclosure of large, open, airy spaces conducive to preventing the spread of the virus.

Another city program is the City's Temporary Bridge Shelters effort, which, as the name suggests, provides a "bridge" for single adults, veterans, and families, currently in temporary shelters until they can find more permanent housing. At the time of this writing, this program consisted of three downtown locations containing 674 beds.

Two other programs designed specifically to provide temporary secure housing for homeless individuals without shelter or simply with no place to store their personal belongings are the City's Homeless Transitional Storage Center and the City's Storage Connect Center. Both sites provide lockers or storage units, and the latter provides restroom facilities on site or help in finding restrooms near the facility.

All the aforementioned programs run by the City of San Diego outsource their actual services under the auspices and support of the City of San Diego, but there are other organizations—generally nonprofits—that operate their own programs for the homeless.

B. Organizations, Institutions, and Businesses

One of the non-governmental entities that operates programs for the homeless is Catholic Charities, USA. This nonprofit has as its emphasis social justice, meaning that it sees as its mission assisting members of society who are otherwise neglected or cast aside by the more fortunate. As such, it considers helping the poor, people of color, and otherwise disadvantaged people and families to be a matter of faith and consistent with its religious belief. As part of its operations, it maintains 35,000 affordable housing units throughout the United States.

Another nonprofit is the Los Angeles House of Ruth. One of the older such organizations, it was founded in 1978, and its main emphasis is helping those fleeing from abusive domestic relationships or mistreatment by employers. As noted earlier, domestic violence is one of the main causes of homelessness and is one of the most tragic causes for both the adult (usually a woman) and the children who suffer lifelong damage from family breakups.

Covenant House of New York, the largest source of help for homeless youth in New York City, is another private agency committed to addressing the problems of homelessness. It pays particular attention to the LGBTQ community and stresses the need for education and advice on building a career. It also provides shelter, medical assistance, as well as other services and help aimed at protecting youth from human trafficking.

C. Individuals

Possibly the greatest impact on reducing homelessness can be had through individual acts of leadership, and there are many ways to do this. A very helpful way to explain how one may show leadership in having a positive impact on homelessness is expressed through the acronym CARE: Contribute, Advocate, Reach Out, and Educate.

One may contribute in numerous ways. The most obvious one, of course, is through financial contributions to one of the organizations mentioned above. But one may also contribute slightly used, clean clothing, especially to those living in unsheltered conditions. That old sweater, jacket, or flannel shirt may have gone out of style, and may seldom be used anymore, but it will make a world of difference to someone trying to stay warm. Or one may have extra household items such as utensils, pots and pans, or small appliances which will make day-to-day living much easier for a homeless family living in meager conditions.

Another way an individual can show leadership in helping the homeless is by *Advocating or* assisting them in convincing government or non-government organizations to develop programs and policies to help the homeless. There are numerous organizations and coalitions which could help the homeless, but they need direction or assistance to bring about change. One can do this through direct personal contact, writing letters to the editor, or enlisting the help of local, state, or national leaders. Or one can address business groups such as Chambers of Commerce, or philanthropic organizations such as Rotary to seek their assistance in helping the homeless.

And then there is the value of *Reaching Out*, or volunteering with one's time in helping the homeless. There is always a need for volunteers at shelters to make life a little easier for those less fortunate in their meager living circumstances. Serve food, distribute clothing, wash dishes, or provide clerical skills to those organizations providing shelter for the homeless.

Finally, there is the need to *Educate* oneself on what it means to be homeless and ways to provide solutions. To assist in doing this there are numerous sources of information such as that provided by the National Alliance to End Homelessness, the National Law Center on Homelessness and Poverty, and the National Health Care for the Homeless Council. After becoming familiar with the issues surrounding homelessness, one can share this information with others to make them aware of it and motivate them to find solutions.

V. Examples of Leadership in Addressing Homelessness

A. Government

An excellent example of government's approach to addressing the homeless issue is the ways in which the Cities of Salt Lake City and San Francisco have addressed it in their ten-year plans from 2005 and 2004 respectively.[15] While there are differences in the cities, primarily in the cost of housing—San Francisco's being much higher than Salt Lake City's—there are similarities. The populations are similar—Salt Lake City was 1.1 million and San Francisco at 850,000 in 2013, and at the start of their ten-year plans each had a homeless population of about 3,000. However, at the end of these plans, the homeless population of San Francisco was about 2,000, whereas that of Salt Lake City was down to 400. What accounts for the difference?

For one thing, Salt Lake City went to great effort in providing decent, in fact, pleasant, supportive housing in a part of the city not typically known for having a great deal of homeless people. This enabled the homeless people in its supportive housing to integrate more successfully with the general population. San Francisco, on the other hand, located its less than pleasant supportive housing in the Tenderloin district of that city, which didn't favor changing the living habits of its homeless tenants.

Also of significance was the degree of counselors' assistance in the two cities. As shown in the figures, Salt Lake City has at least twice the ratio of counselors to residents as San Francisco, the former having fifteen residents for each counselor, whereas the latter has about thirty for each counselor. Clearly, the counseling attention paid the residents can be much more effective in Salt Lake City than San Francisco.

Perhaps of greatest significance in the approach of the two cities to their shared problem is the degree of effective leadership in the homeless programs existing in each city. In Salt Lake City the director of the state's homeless programs is Lloyd Pendleton, who brings a commonsense, positive attitude to the city's effort to address the issue of homelessness. As he's stated, "It's not rocket science. Homeless people need housing. Give it to them. And give them counseling." Part of the reason for his success is probably the fact that prior to serving in his current position, he had been the director of international charity programs for the Mormon Church. Regardless of the source of his leadership capability, the success of Salt Lake City's approach to solving its homeless challenge must be attributed to some extent to the leadership of Lloyd Pendleton.

B. Businesses and Organizations

An excellent example of what businesses can do to advocate for the homeless is the Third Door Coalition. In response to a tax increase in Seattle in 2018, which was intended to build housing for the homeless, several businesses and nonprofit organizations formed the Third Door Coalition. This nonprofit group of business leaders envisioned an alternate path to addressing the issue of chronic homelessness, one which was based on the strategies they've used to be successful in business.

Among these alternatives was a plan to develop and build 6,500 units of supportive housing over a five-year period at a cost of $1.676 million, and to finance this effort the business leaders apportioned revenue development with the state contributing 20 percent, King County 30 percent, cities in the county 10 percent, and the remaining 40 percent coming from the leaders themselves. This insured that businesses had a stake in the plan, as they considered helping the chronically homeless good for their own success and that of the community.

Central to the success of the Third Door Coalition's approach to addressing this challenge of providing housing to the homeless in Seattle was its emphasis on the concepts of Housing First and Permanent Supportive Housing.[16] A pillar of these programs was the belief that any planned housing should not require the chronically homeless to meet qualifications such as commitment to training or agreement to certain behavioral changes. Rather, emphasis should be addressing the immediate needs of the homeless, that is, finding them a permanent, decent place to live. This, in turn, was based on the psychologist Abraham Maslow's hierarchy of needs, which recognizes the inherent psychological need of every human being to have certain very basic requirements satisfied before any, more complex, needs can be addressed as shown in Figure 4-1. In other words, a person has to have such basic needs such as food, water, breathing, and shelter satisfied before he or she can aspire to such goals as safety, belonging, and self-esteem.[17] In other words, before one can address the other requirements of simply being human, he or she has to have certain basic needs satisfied. And this is the goal of the business leaders in the Third Door Coalition.

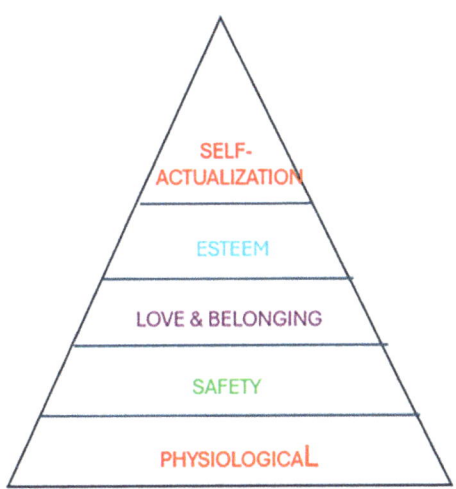

Figure 4-1. Maslow's Hierarchy of Needs.

The success of this approach has been verified in many cities and government programs throughout the country.[18] In general, there's a significant reduction in emergency room expenses where permanent supportive housing is available. When someone has a place to live, and there is health care provided, or at least information on where it can be provided, it is less likely for those who would otherwise be homeless to seek emergency care services. Contributing to this is the fact that 90 percent of those in Supportive Housing or Permanent Supportive Housing (SH/PSH) are likely to remain housed after one year versus only 35 percent of those who are not. As a result, there is a significant financial savings in programs which implement Permanent Supportive Housing.

Due to the leadership of the business leaders who found the Third Door Coalition, and are actively involved, the chronically homeless of Seattle have an alternative not otherwise available through government programs.

C. Individual

Probably no other single individual has contributed more to care for the homeless than Father Joe Carroll in San Diego. Born in the Bronx in 1940, he came to San Diego in 1963 and was ordained a Catholic priest in 1974. In 1982 the Bishop of San Diego was looking for someone to take over the St. Vincent de Paul Center—the Diocese's homeless facility—and someone recommended Father Joe. In describing Father Joe to the Bishop, he said "He can squeeze money out of a rock."[19] This was to become the most distinguishing leadership characteristic of Father Joe–his ability to raise funds to fulfill his vision of solving the homeless crisis in San Diego.

His vision was to provide a single point at which a homeless person or family could not only find a decent place to live, but one where they could find medical care, employment assistance, and the basic necessities of life. Explaining this on a TV interview, he told the interviewer, "Housing is not the answer to homelessness," but the solution requires so much more.[20] Except for raising money, Father Joe is best known for the concept of one-stop shopping, which provides for food, clothing, housing, and medical care in one place.

Father Joe has been so successful at doing this (providing many services in addition to housing) that St. Vincent de Paul has grown into Father Joe's Villages, which includes Martha's Village and Kitchen, the Toussaint Academy, and the Joan Kroc Center. Through his leadership, no one has done more for the homeless in San Diego than Father Joe Carroll.

References

1. National Alliance to END HOMELESSNESS, *Changes in the HUD Definition of "Homelessness."*
2. National Alliance to END HOMELESSNESS, *What Causes Homelessness?*
3. Cara Brumfield, *Counting People Experiencing Homelessness*, ECONOMIC SECURITY and OPPORTUNITY INITIATIVE, September 17, 2018.
4. *State of Homelessness: 2020 Edition*, National Alliance to End Homelessness.
5. Mathew Desmond, *Evicted*, 2016, Crown Publishers, New York.
6. *State of Homelessness, 2023 Edition.*
7. Esteban Ortiz-Ospina and Max Roser, *Homelessness*, Our World in Data.

8. Christopher Johnson, *Socio-economic and Environmental Impact of Homelessness in Olympia, Washington*, Environmental Health and Social Justice, March 3, 2016.
9. Scott Wilson, *Hepatitis A outbreak among homeless a byproduct of California's housing crunch*, Washington Post, October 25, 2017.
10. Gabriel Petek, *The 2020–21 Budget: The Governor's Homelessness Plan*, Feb 11, 2020.
11. Jacob Passy, *Nearly Half of the US's Homeless People Live in one State: California*, MarketWatch, Sept. 29, 2019.
12. Petek, *The 2020–21 Budget*.
13. *City of San Diego's Homeless Shelters and Services Programs—SDHC*.
14. *Building a Movement to End Homelessness*, National Coalition for the Homeless.
15. Kevin Fagan, *What S.F. can learn from Salt Lake City*. San Francisco Chronicle, June 28, 2014.
16. Third Door Coalition, *Introduction to Housing First/Permanent Supportive Housing*.
17. Saul McLeod, *Maslow's Hierarchy of Needs*, Simply Psychology, Dec. 29, 2020.
18. Third Door Coalition, *The Effectiveness of Housing First & Permanent Supportive Housing*.
19. John Wilkens, *Father Joe celebrates his 70th birthday—and retirement*, San Diego Union Tribune.
20. *10News Exclusive: Father Joe discusses homelessness in San Diego*, SAN DIEGO KGTV, Oct. 26, 2019.

5

Leadership in Social Equity— Food and Nutrition Insecurity

I. Definitions and Background

A. Definitions

According to the Food and Agriculture Organization (FAO), "there exists the right of everyone to have access to safe and nutritious food, consistent with the right to adequate food and the fundamental right of everyone to be free from hunger."[1] More specifically, the same World Food Summit states, "Food security exists when all people, at all times, have physical and economic access to sufficient safe and nutritious food that meets their dietary needs and food preferences for an active and healthy life."

Again, according to the FAO, there needs to be four definitions of food security for it to exist: physical *availability* of food, economic and physical *access* to food, food *utilization*, and *stability* of these dimensions over time.[2]

With regard to *availability*, this condition assumes that all the factors of producing food, such as sufficient land for crops, water for irrigation, and healthy livestock are present and thriving to produce food. This condition also assumes that weather, climactic and political circumstances are such that these factors can result in the production of food.

Even then, economic conditions may exist in a nation or among certain groups of its people so that they do not have *access* to this food. In remote regions of Africa, indigenous people may not have access to financial resources to purchase any food that is produced, or they may be located too far from areas where the food is produced and sold. So, while there is theoretically food available for a nation's people, conditions may exist which prevent large parts of its population from being food secure.

Even in those cases when all of a nation's people have access to some type of basic food, it might be the case that *utilization* of this food does not meet the requirements of safe and healthy nutrition. The result may then be infectious disease, stunted growth, or, in the worst case, *wasting*, in which the physical condition of poor nutrition, such as distended bellies, is evident.

But a nation's people cannot be considered food secure without *stability*, even if all these conditions are satisfied at least periodically. In other words, these conditions must be met over time. It's not enough for there to be enough food only during a good growing season, or when there's sufficient rainfall, or when the population has enough income to satisfy its need for nourishment. There must be always available enough nutritious food to satisfy a healthy, growing population.

Food security is not just a matter of having and eating enough food. Of equal or greater importance to good health and well-being is eating the right kinds of food, or good nutrition. One element of food being nutritious is its inclusion of the basic food groups: 1) fruits and vegetables; 2) whole grains; 3) meat and beans; 4) milk and dairy; and 5) fats and oils. Beyond these, of course, is the issue of how your body achieves nutrition from these basic groups, or how these food groups provide the necessary *nutrients* to the body. Specifically, these nutrients are: 1) proteins; 2) carbohydrates; 3) fats; 4) vitamins and minerals; and 5) water. These elements are the necessary elements of good nutrition. Without good nutrition, even though there is some basic food or food supplement available, the conditions for food and nutrition security cannot be met.

B. Effects of Food and Nutrition Insecurity

While malnutrition includes several conditions of food availability and consumption, actually including obesity and overweight, the most relevant physical conditions with regard to food insecurity are *underweight*, *stunting*, and *wasting*. These conditions manifest themselves in all the poor health and societal abnormalities traditionally observed in those who, for whatever reason, go hungry.

An underweight child is one who has a low weight for their age, whereas a stunted child (or adult) is one with a low height for their age, and a wasted person (usually a child) is one with a low weight for their height.[3] All of these conditions are relative, and somewhat arbitrary, but in their extreme, they are a result of food and nutrition insecurity. The wasted child, perhaps with a distended stomach from the lack of any nutritious food, is indicative of the seriousness of this worldwide problem. While 47 million children under the age of five are considered wasted, there are 14.3 million children who are "severely wasted."[4]

All of these are the outward signs of food and nutrition insecurity. One aspect that is often taken for granted is hunger. Even in developed nations there are pockets of the population that frequently go hungry due to the lack of food or a health sustaining diet. In many large cities children go to school on empty stomachs and depend on school lunch programs at minimal cost. And during times of crises, such as the COVID-19 pandemic worldwide in 2020, there were lengthy food lines in otherwise moderately advanced socioeconomic areas of the United States.

C. Causes of Food and Nutrition Insecurity

It is important to distinguish between the causes of food insecurity in Third World countries, and in the United States and other developed countries. For various reasons, primarily the difference in economic development, social norms, and governance between the two, the causes are different, and the solutions vary. The differences among countries with varying levels of income is evident in the degree to which percentages of the population are food insecure, as shown in Figure 5-1.

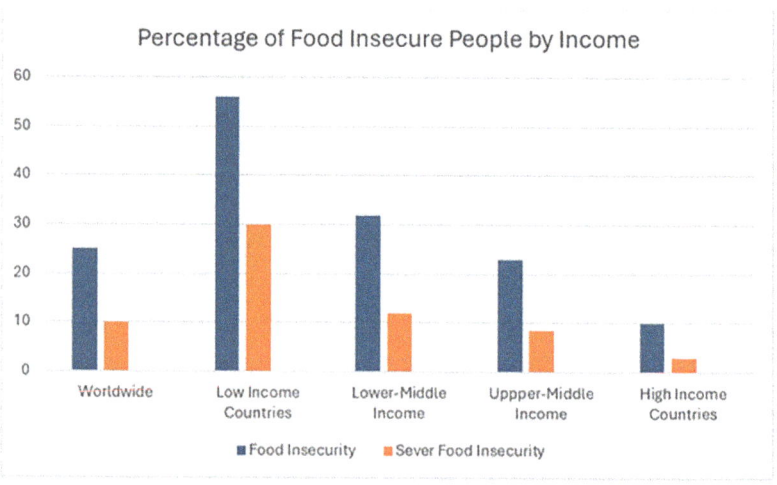

Figure 5-1 Percentages of food insecure people by income.
USDA Economic Research Service

Chief among the causes of food insecurity in these countries is *poverty*, and as a result their people cannot afford basic subsistence, to say nothing of nourishing food. In many cases desperate subsistence farmers sell off their livestock and other possessions just to feed their families, and not only do they starve, but they lose the means by which to provide for their families in the future. The result is a spiraling descent into the most severe food insecurity. A particularly stark example is the Democratic Republic of Congo, where most of its population lives on less than $1.25 a day, but there are other causes as well.[5]

Among these other causes are *food shortages* in which growing seasons are interrupted due to social unrest, natural disasters, or great distances between the sources of food and those who need it. More typical of underdeveloped nations in Africa and Asia where irrigation and advanced agricultural methods (especially fertilizer) are less available, food shortages are sometimes the cause of food insecurity in developed countries as well, but not as frequently.

A more common cause of food shortages in Africa and the Middle East is *war and conflict*. Typical of this is the ongoing civil war in Yemen in which half its population needs food. Another example is in South Sudan where civil war in 2017 has led to famine in two of its regions, the UN Food and Agriculture Organization has characterized food shortages there as unprecedented, and 40 percent of the country is in dire need of food assistance. The civil war in Syria, which began in 2011, has caused the displacement of more than half its population—some 12 million people—and it has killed hundreds of thousands and led to ongoing food shortages throughout the conflict.[6]

Potentially the most serious threat to food security that exists now and will likely become greater in the years to come, is climate change. Rising sea levels in small island nations, and farms located near the continental coasts, as in Bangladesh, totally obliterate small farms. And as temperatures continue to rise, crops that prospered when it was cooler are no longer able to survive. With the rise in temperature, droughts become more frequent, and subsistence farmers without irrigation can no longer raise crops for food. Once fertile fields often become deserts due to the lack of rainfall and soil amendment. And, when rainfall does come, it's often in the form of deluges that can entirely wipe out newly planted fields. The result is severe food insecurity in nations unable to grow lifesaving food.

Related to climate change and the ability to raise food is *good nutrition*. Much of the population in Africa and Asia rely on one or two staple crops, such as wheat or rice, and even when climate conditions are right to produce these crops, these people do not have access to the vitamins and minerals in fruits and vegetables that are conducive to healthy lives.

Another contributing factor to food insecurity is *poor public policy*. How stable are the existing governments in Third World nations? Even if stable, what is the attitude of the existing governments to providing food security to their people? Can a government beset with corruption be expected to concern itself with the food security of its citizens? The frequent civil unrest in nations such as Myanmar in Southeast Asia, the Sudan in Africa, and the northern triangle of Central America are testimony to the lack of regard the governments of El Salvador, Honduras, and Guatemala have for the government's role in caring for its citizens.

Something not as common in the developed nations as it is in those less developed is *gender inequality*. Because of this inequality, women are often left to till the families' fields, search for and transport scarce water for sanitation, and raise children with little or no say in the responsibilities of families. The result is a very uneven distribution of labor in families, more children than the families can support, and a consequent shortage of nutritious food for many families living in Third World countries.

One more cause of world hunger and food insecurity is *forced migration*, which is unique in that not only is it a cause of hunger, but itself is caused by populations suffering from food insecurity. As already noted, the civil wars in Syria and Yemen were largely the result of their peoples being unable to feed themselves, and this led them to flee in search of food security. But such migration itself disrupted efforts to grow food, raise livestock, and otherwise provide people with ways to feed their families. Such forced migrations have occurred all over the world, including families fleeing from northern Africa across the Mediterranean into Europe and Central America from which thousands have fled across Mexico, seeking asylum in the United States.

Yes, there are numerous reasons for which hunger and food insecurity is common among Third World and lower socioeconomic countries. But there is also food and nutrition insecurity in the more advanced socioeconomic countries of Europe and North America. Even in the United States, which by most estimates is the envy of the world for its ability to feed its citizens, there is significant food and nutrition insecurity. While the causes and effects of such food insecurity are somewhat different from lower socioeconomic countries, the human costs are, in some respects, just as devastating.

As noted, the issue of food insecurity differs in the United States and developed countries from that internationally. While some of the basic causes, such as poverty, are similar to those internationally, there are many people living in lower socioeconomic countries who endure conditions that are just nonexistent in the U.S., such as war and conflict and forced migration.

By far the most significant cause of food insecurity in the United States is poverty. While poverty has always been a major cause of food insecurity, its significance has become clearer during the COVID-19 pandemic of 2020. Among the many debilitating effects of the pandemic, job loss and the impact on peoples' lives, especially food insecurity, were the most damaging.[7]

While millions of households experienced income loss, almost no households with incomes above $75,000 experienced low food security. And yet, food lines throughout the United States were overwhelmed during the pandemic with cars lined up simply trying to provide food for their families. While poverty has always been a major cause of food insecurity in the United States, its impact was more evident during the pandemic of 2020. And while poverty is the common denominator for food insecurity among both developed and Third World countries, there are other causes of food insecurity in the United States.

One of these is the existence of "food deserts." Generally occurring in urban areas, "a food dessert is a place where it is difficult to find and purchase enough healthy, nutritious food to meet dietary needs."[8] Given this demographic, about 22.5 percent of the people in these areas who were food insecure are African American, and 18.5 percent are Hispanic, which compares with the national average of 12.3 percent. A major effect of this food insecurity among all people living in these "food deserts" is an increase in both diabetes and obesity resulting from not having access to fresh fruits and vegetables. Particularly affected by food security in these areas are children, who bear the lifelong physical and mental effects of not having enough nutritious food. Nationally, a 2018 study showed that 18 percent of children are food insecure.

Natural disasters are another cause of food insecurity, including hurricanes, wildfires, and tornadoes, which affect both the ability to raise healthy foods on farms and supply disruptions. During the summer of 2018 the author was flying into Omaha, Nebraska, and was astonished at the amount of farmland which was still under water from storms which occurred weeks before. During the summer and fall of 2020, food lines extending for what appeared to be miles were filled with families seeking food during the COVID-19 pandemic.

Ironically, while a good portion of the world suffers from food insecurity because it can't provide itself with even the basic foods, a serious problem in the United States is it's addiction to junk and processed foods.[9] These foods—using the term loosely—are generally characterized by their added sugar, salt, and fats, which have been associated with certain types of cancer, diabetes, heart disease, and, of course, obesity. Moreover, they are designed for overconsumption, and considered addicting, hence the term "sugar high." And the negative effects of consuming added sugar in processed or junk foods has been demonstrated in study after study. One such study in Spain found a 51 percent increase in depression due to sugar's effects on the central nervous system. And sugar's effect on the endocrine and cardiovascular systems is an increase in diabetes and obesity. Also, given that the targets of junk food are mostly children, it's significant that Australian researchers have found a greater susceptibility to some diseases among younger people which may be related to eating more such junk foods. Certainly, this type of food insecurity is every bit as harmful as not having enough food to eat.

II. Extent Worldwide and in U.S.

A. Worldwide

As noted, there is a significant difference in the causes, effects, and extent of food insecurity between the developed and undeveloped nations of the world. This becomes clear when one considers the extent of food insecurity in the nations of Africa.[10] The Percentages of Undernourishment (PoU) in all regions of the continent except northern Africa are projected to increase drastically from 2018 to 2030, at which time it had been hoped for these regions in Africa and the Middle East to have met the United Nations Sustainability goals.

The reasons for this are several. First, the economic performance of the nations in these regions are not nearly what they are in more developed nations, even in parts of Asia, and most certainly in Europe and the U.S. This is reflected in less farm mechanization, irrigation, fewer access roads to deliver farm products, and the use of fertilizer to grow them.

Secondly, wars and conflict are almost a part of life in these regions. The strife in Syria during the first part of the twenty-first century is most typical of the effect war has had on food security in that nation, and tribal conflicts affecting food availability are typical in Sudan and Ethiopia.

Finally, the effects of climate change reflected in frequent drought, desertification, and unreliable growing seasons which limit the growth of crops, are major causes of food insecurity in these regions.

The effects of such food insecurity differ also between these undeveloped and developed nations. Whereas in the west such food insecurity does cause considerable pain and suffering, almost nowhere in developed nations does one see children with distended stomachs resulting from the lack of food, such as one sees in the undeveloped nations of Africa and the Middle East. Nor does one see the spread of infectious disease caused by malnutrition as exists in Africa and the Middle East.

B. Food Insecurity in the U.S.

Prior to the COVID-19 pandemic of 2020, 10.5 percent or 13.7 million American households in the U.S. were considered to be food insecure. Moreover, one-third of these were deemed so food insecure that they couldn't find food of any kind to eat, and households with children were 1.5 times as likely to be food insecure as those with without. And as Figure 5-2 shows, people of color (African Americans, Hispanics mostly) were significantly more insecure than others.

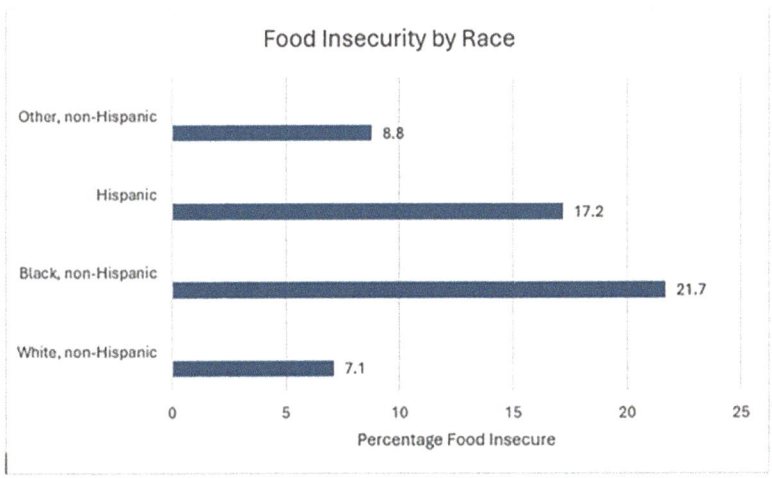

Figure 5-2 Food Insecurity Percentages by Race in 2020. Source: Center for American Progress

After the coronavirus pandemic of 2020 these percentages of food insecure households increased to 27.5 percent, which was borne out every day on the nightly news which showed long lines of cars waiting to receive food for their families.

III. Sustainable Development Impact

A. The Future of Food on Sustainable Development[11]

In general, there are two major considerations determining the sustainability of food worldwide: the ability to feed a growing population given the earth's *environmental space*,[18] and the way in which we produce food today.

The first of these, environmental space, "recognizes a limit to the level of resources each person can consume if society is to be environmentally sustainable."[12] Environmental space, in turn, consists of several factors. As the world's population increases, currently at about 7.7 billion (in 2021) and expected to increase to about 11 billion by the end of the century, it is expected by the UN Food and Agricultural Organization that the demand for food will increase by 70 percent by the year 2050. Unfortunately, the land available to support this increasing demand for food is limited.

Compounding this decreasing amount of land available to grow food is the increase in soil erosion for various reasons, for example, drought, overuse of fertilizers, flooding, and so on. This is especially true in China and India, where 22,000 square miles of land is becoming desert every year for these reasons. Such "desertification" has led to the loss of one-third of the arable land area on earth.[13]

As the demand for food production increases, not only is there a greater demand for arable land, but there is also a growing demand for water. As this demand increases, nations have drawn more and more water from aquifers, leading to their depletion. As a result of the increased demand for water for use in irrigation, the water tables in China and India especially have been dropping. In the United States, the Ogallala Aquifer, which provides irrigation for much of the Midwest's agriculture, has been losing 1.3 trillion gallons of water greater than rainfall can replenish.

The other major consideration influencing the sustainability of the world's food supply, especially in the United States, is the way in which we grow, distribute, and consume food. Artificial "enhancements" to the soil is an integral part of the way we produce our food supply everywhere in the world, but especially in the United States. To compensate for periodic droughts and the degradation of soil, large agri-businesses resort to pesticides, fertilizers, and other chemicals to increase crop yields. Ironically, these often degrade the life of the soil, and more such artificial means are then required to preserve its health, which results in further degradation in a never-ending cycle. Fertilizer runoff frequently enters rivers and streams, and eventually the ocean, which creates aquatic "dead zones" through a process termed eutrophication.

And with the growth in world population and the increased demand for food, farming is being replaced by large centrally located agri-businesses. Especially in the Middle East and Africa, the means of production are often located far from population growth centers, which limits the people's access to healthy food. And as these agri-businesses become larger they are able to minimize their costs to the detriment of smaller farms which might grow healthier foods and distribute them locally.

With the growth of such large agri-businesses and their attempts to minimize costs, there is the explosion of processed foods which have become more and more the staples of people everywhere. Ultimately, the effect is an increase in less than healthy food, with a reduction in the sustainable physical and mental health of populations everywhere.

B. Food Security's Impact on Sustainable Development

The effect of food security, at its core, is its effect on the physical and mental development of human beings. Without access to sufficient and nutritious food, the human body cannot grow and evolve to become the functioning, achieving, reproducing members of the human race. This effect begins during our prenatal existence, when the access of the mother to sufficient and nutritious food is critical and extends throughout life. Perhaps more important is the effect of food security on mental development. This is most evident in all countries where children are sent off to school with empty stomachs. This is simply not conducive to social and mental development. One strategy to address this is the practice in many American schools where they offer free or heavily subsidized breakfasts and lunches to all children regardless of their ability to pay.

C. Sustainable Development's Impact on Food Security

Almost important as the effect of food insecurity on sustainable development is the effect of sustainable development on food security. This is most clearly illustrated in the United Nations Sustainable Development Goals for 2015–2030.

Working through the United Nations in 2015, 193 nations announced 17 Sustainable Development Goals that were to guide global development for the world over the period from 2015 to 2030. Almost all these goals bore some relationship to food and nutrition security, but at least eight of them affected it directly.[14] The first of these—End Poverty (Goal Number 1)—bears a direct relationship to food security because it is the most common cause of food insecurity, both worldwide and in the United States. Another way to look at it is the fact the producers of food include small farms in rural areas who often live from one season to another just hoping to grow enough food to feed their families.

The second UN Goal—End Hunger (Goal 2)—is even more direct in that it addresses the most basic aspect of food insecurity, not having enough food of any kind to eat. This is most common in African nations or the Middle East, which cannot procure even the simplest kind of food to stave off the real physical pain from not having a minimal amount of food to eat. But the effect on sustainable development is also seen in developed nations in which children go to school hungry and cannot concentrate because they are unable to think of anything except how hungry they really are.

Another way in which one of the UN's Sustainable Development Goals affects food security is the role played by not having enough access to water (Goal 6) to grow food. At least 70 percent of all water withdrawn from the earth is used to grow food. While not as consequential as other causes of food insecurity, not having enough water for sanitation and preparing food is a contributing factor in food and nutrition security.

Similarly, Energy (Goal 7) is a major determinant of the ability to produce and distribute food. The UN's Food and Agriculture Organization estimates that energy constitutes approximately 30 percent of the cost of food production systems. This includes the energy in mechanized agriculture, food processing, and transporting food products. As the world's population grows and there is more demand for food, the need for, and cost of, energy increase.

Currently, the world wastes about a third of the food it produces. Sustainable Development Goal 12—Sustainable Consumption and Production—addresses this wasted food both on the farm and in processing to ensure that the otherwise wasted food is available for food security. Steps such as food wasted in preparation, serving portions of food left uneaten, or failure to monitor the life of various foods result in unnecessary food waste that could feed the world's growing population.

Especially in parts of the world affected by drought, excessive rainfall, desertification, and other climate events, the UN Sustainable Development Goal 13—Combat Climate change—addresses the need to account for climate in producing food. Obliviously, agriculture is an industry most affected by changes in climate, and steps to account for, or mitigate, the effects of these changes are necessary to feed the world's growing population and prevent food insecurity.

Almost 3 billion of the world's people currently receive 20 percent of their protein from seafood. Unfortunately, about 29 percent of the commercial fish stocks are overfished, leading to a possible scarcity of this source of protein for much of the world. Sustainable Development Goal 14—Oceans, Seas, and Marine Resources—addresses this potential scarcity. One of the steps taken is the development of aquacultures to manage the growth of these fisheries, and this is currently the fastest growing food sector. Especially significant is the growth of an industry to produce a healthy food source in an environmentally sustainable way.

Finally, both farmland and forests have an influence on the food we eat through Sustainable Develop Goal 15—Life on Land. Currently, with the degradation of farmland, almost 75 percent of crop genetic diversity has been lost and 22 percent of animal breeds on these lands are endangered; with the deforestation in the Amazon and other forests, indigenous people lose both their sources of biodiversity and sources of food.

IV. Leadership Opportunities to Address Food Insecurity

A. Government

Probably the best example of government leadership in addressing food instability is the Supplemental Nutrition Assistance Program (SNAP), a U.S. federal program administered by the states. The program is intended to feed families which are 130 percent above the poverty level get through difficult times. In 2015 these included 4.6 million Americans, of whom two million were children, and 366,000 were seniors, both of which are vulnerable populations.

Aside from enabling families to feed themselves, SNAP is also good for the economy. One study in 2010 showed that for every $1 billion increase in SNAP funding there were 8,900 to 17,000 jobs created.[15]

B. Businesses and Organizations

The nonprofit *Feeding America* operates a network of 200 food banks and 60,000 food pantries through all the states and Puerto Rico. These food banks are staffed by volunteers and provide leadership opportunities to those wishing to assist the food insecure.

Similarly, Meals on Wheels is another nonprofit which delivers food to seniors and those otherwise homebound who have difficulty in providing food for themselves. As of 2020, volunteers provided 221 million meals to 2.4 million seniors each year. In addition to providing nutritious meals to those in need, volunteers often provide the only social connection to many seniors who live alone and can serve as an alert for assistance to seniors and others they are accustomed to seeing on their route, but who don't answer their door. Again, the Meals on Wheels organization is providing practical leadership in helping feed the food insecure.

C. Individuals

There are numerous opportunities for individuals to exercise leadership in helping the food insecure. As just mentioned, numerous nonprofits are staffed entirely by volunteers and provide a relatively easy way to get directly involved in a leadership endeavor.

V. Examples of Leadership in Addressing Food Insecurity

A. Government

An excellent example of a federal government program that has been an unqualified success in addressing food insecurity throughout the world is *Feed the Future*. Consisting of several federal agencies, the program has since its beginning in 2011 been responsible for lifting 23.4 million people out of poverty and preventing stunting in 3.4 million children. What's more, its efforts have generated $413.7 billion in agricultural sales in the years 2011–2019.[16]

The reasons for its success are many and provide lessons for how such federal programs not only demonstrate the value of leadership in conducting foreign aid, but also how these lessons can be applied to other such programs in conducting foreign policy.

One of the reasons for the success of this program is the fact that it involves multiple federal agencies and has been a cooperative effort between the executive branch and Congress. Such cooperation among agencies and between the executive and legislative branches has made it a bipartisan effort. Of course, leadership in both the executive and legislative branches has ensured such cooperation.

Secondly, the program has focused on twelve countries in Africa, Asia, Latin American and the Middle East. This focus has allowed the federal government to target the worst examples of food insecurity in these countries.

Finally, the program has worked with local governments in each of the targeted countries, thus avoiding possible interference or even corruption by the central governments. By doing this and facilitating the support of donors in the U.S., the program has ensured that food assistance gets to where it is most needed and is not diverted to corrupt leaders.

The success of *Feed the Future* can serve as a model for other foreign aid programs by the U.S. government. The mass migrations from El Salvador, Honduras, and Guatemala in the first part of the twenty-first century were motivated by issues similar to those successfully addressed by *Feed the Future*. Perhaps the best way to begin to restore some sense of order at the U.S. southern border is to address the root causes of the mass migrations from these countries, and among these root causes is food insecurity among the people of Central America.

B. Businesses and Other Organizations—World Central Kitchen[17]

It would be hard to find a better example of a business or nonprofit organization that exemplifies more the spirit of "feeding the hungry" than Jose Andres' World Central Kitchen. In 2010 following the 2010 magnitude 7.0 earthquake in Haiti, Andres went there with the intention of installing cook stoves throughout the country to help the nation feed itself. At the same time his vision of establishing a nonprofit to empower people to develop the skills necessary to feed themselves took hold. From this vision he founded the *World Central Kitchen,* which had as its mission the advance of education, health, jobs, and social enterprise.

Part of this mission was establishing a network of 140 chefs who, in turn, operated and taught at schools. By 2016 the chefs working with local people had established fifty cooking schools in Haiti using efficient cook stoves and had plans for establishing forty more schools in that nation. Incidentally, this early connection with Haiti was to remain the focal point of the World Central Kitchen.

Indeed, this early experience with feeding the hungry after the 2010 Haiti earthquake led to disaster relief in the following years, including Hurricane Matthew in Haiti in 2016, Hurricane Harvey in Houston in 2017, Hurricane Maria in Puerto Rico in 2017, and Hurricane Dorian in 2019. For various reasons, the nonprofit also provided food assistance to the Dominican Republic, Nicaragua, Zambia, Peru, Cuba, Uganda, and Cambodia. While the World Central Kitchen is best known for addressing hunger and food insecurity throughout the developing world, its mission to empower local populations and provide jobs while doing so cannot be overemphasized. At home, Andres lobbied Congress to provide aid to U.S. restaurants and appoint a "food czar" but, unfortunately, was not immediately successful. As he said while attempting to do this "We know how to fix our food issues. What we lack is the leadership." How appropriate from one who is so well-known for using his leadership in addressing food insecurity throughout the world!

C. Individual leadership[18]

Illustrating the fact that one does not have to be older to demonstrate leadership in any endeavor is Nikkia Rhodes, a twenty-three-year-old chef in Louisville, Kentucky. Influenced by her mother and grandmother who volunteered for Volunteers of America in feeding the homeless, Nikkia not only wanted to help the less fortunate, but wanted to learn everything she could about the culinary arts. While still in high school she attended classes at a community college to learn everything she could about food preparation and being a chef. Shortly after graduation she started a culinary arts program at a local high school, using an ordinary desk as a cutting board. She continued to improve the course over several years until the high school built a state-of-the-art teaching kitchen in 2019, which operated until the pandemic in 2020.

In the early days of the pandemic, by some estimates Louisville's best-known chef, Edward Lee, wanted to start a nonprofit dedicated to feeding mostly poorer African Americans in the Louisville area. Even though Rhodes was only twenty-three at the time, Lee selected her and some of her high school friends to staff it. Also, they named the nonprofit the McAtee Community Kitchen, after David McAtee, a local chef who had recently been killed by the National Guard protesting the death of Breonna Taylor. Prior to that, he himself was active in providing food for the less fortunate, and so it was appropriate for the new center be named after him. Rhodes used all the professional and leadership skills she had learned over the last five years in making the McAtee Community Kitchen a life saver for the food insecure during the pandemic, providing food for 250 families of four three days a week. In doing so she was able to employ her leadership skills and passion for providing food security for the benefit of those less fortunate at a time of critical need for her community and the nation.

References

1. *Rome Declaration on World Food Security*, WORLD FOOD SUMMIT, 13–17 November, 1996, Rome, Italy,
2. *Food Security Policy Brief*, FAO, June, 2006,
3. *Key Facts*, World Health Organization, April 1, 2020,
4. Key Facts, WHO,
5. *THE TOP 10 CAUSES OF WORLD HUNGER*, CONCERN worldwide US, May 27, 2019
6. Zachary Laub, *Syria's Civil War: The Descent Into Horror*, February 19, 2020, Council on Foreign Relations.
7. Lauren Bauer, *Hungary at Thanksgiving: A Fall 2020 Update on Food Insecurity in the U.S.*, November 23, 2020, Brookings Institution,
8. Lisa Jubilee, *Food Inequality in America: What Living in A "Food Desert" Looks Like, June 19, 2020*, Living Proof,
9. Liz Meszaros, *Processed and Junk Foods: Bad news for pretty much every system in the body*, October 23, 2018, MDLinx,
10. *2020 TRANSFORMING FOOD SYSTEMS FOR AFFORDABLE HEALTHY DIETS*, Food and Agriculture Organization of the United Nations Rome, 2020,
11. Prince Charles, On the Future of Food, May 4, 2011, THE PRINCE'S SPEECH.
12. Andres R. Edwards, The Sustainability Revolution, 2005, New Society Publishers.
13. *Withgott, Jay, and Brennan, Scott, Essential Environment—The Science Behind the Stories, 3rd Ed., Benjamin Cummings, 2009.*
14. *FAO and the 17 Sustainable Development Goals*, FAO, 2015.
15. *Understanding SNAP, the Supplemental Nutrition Assistance Program*, Feeding America.
16. Daniel V. Speckhard, *Feed the Future: After a decade of success,*

let's make it better, Atlantic Council, Oct. 1, 2020.
17. Monica Burton, *The Story Behind the José Andrés Nonprofit Serving Hurricane Dorian Victim,* Sept. 5, 2019, Eater.
18. Adrian Miller, A Louisville Community Kitchen Aims to Heal a Divide. Its Best-Known Chef and a Rising Star Are Behind It, July 8, 2020, RESY.

6

Poverty and Income Inequality

I. Definitions and Background

A. Poverty

The issues of poverty and income inequality are related and overlap for many reasons, and there are so many unique challenges for leadership. Poverty can exist for many reasons other than inadequate income and each precipitating cause of poverty presents its own need for leadership. Consideration of the many aspects of poverty is helpful.

In general, poverty is the condition of not having the basic necessities of life – usually expressed in terms of income or wealth. According to the World Bank, though, poverty is defined for an individual either as moderate or living on $1.90 to $3.10 per day, or extreme, as living on less than $1.90 a day.[1] Other terms which describe poverty are *absolute poverty* which pertains to those whose incomes fall below a certain country-specific level, and *relative poverty*, which pertains to those whose incomes fall a certain percentage—usually 50 percent—below the median income for the country in which they live.

But poverty isn't just about money. Rather, it's about having the basic necessities of life. The UN recognizes this and assigns a *Multidimensional Poverty Index (MPI)* to countries in accordance with how well their population fares in three necessities of life areas: Health, Education, and Standard of Living. Among ten indicators included are school attendance, nutrition, drinking water, electricity, housing, and other similar life necessities. While the extent of poverty is quantified with monetary values such as so much per capita per day, the real effect of poverty is the impact it has on the ability to attain even the most basic items for life.

In addition to these very real effects of poverty, there are certain less tangible, but nonetheless real, aspects or effects.[2] These fall under the general heading of *subjugation*, or the act of looking down on, or minimizing, those who are affected by poverty. Due to their poverty, society often excludes them from participation in, and giving them a voice in, community events and decisions. In other words, their opinions and contributions are not considered as worthy as the ones from those more fortunate. Similarly, those experiencing poverty are frequently socially isolated for many of the same reasons. Others simply don't want to associate with others they deem to be "beneath them." And this is not to discount the isolating effects of the very real shame felt by those in poverty. Somehow, they equate their worth as persons with the assets they have or don't have, and this takes a toll on their self-esteem. As a result, government (and society) unconsciously (or consciously) withholds many of the resources given to those with more of everything, such as better schools, parks, and services (think, Flint, Michigan). All these less than tangible aspects of poverty combine to make attractive work and employment less available to those who have less than those who have more.

There are also aspects of poverty, termed *aggravators*, which make poverty even worse by compounding its negative effects. Among these is *racism*. Being the victim of racism is a terrible thing, but for those living in poverty that condition is worse for those considered less worthy of respect because of the color of their skin.

Another aggravator for those in poverty is the potential issue of the *social identity* of those living in poverty. For those who are members of the LGBQT (Lesbian, Gay, Bi-sexual, Queer, Transgender) community, the ostracism they might experience because of this social identity is compounded by living in poverty. And of course, the longer a person lives in poverty the more difficult to escape its hold on him or her becomes. Finally, the *accumulation of aspects* in which the person living in poverty may experience all these aggravators, and the pain and embarrassment of living in poverty are cumulative.

This begs the question of what are the causes of poverty. While there are many, the United Nations Organization for the Coordination of Human Affairs (OCHA) has identified at least nine.[3] Some of these are more appropriate for Third World or undeveloped countries, but many apply to the United States as well.

Perhaps not surprisingly, one of these is inability to access clean water and food. But a moment's thought reveals that a hungry person or one without access to potable water for drinking or basic sanitation is probably unable to care for himself or family. Without the energy provided by food, or the water needed for basic health, a person is unable to do the things they need to do to ward off poverty. And if there is access to water, it may be so far away, or difficult to access, that there is little time left to engage in work to avoid poverty.

Related to inadequate access to water and food is the unavailability of employment to earn a decent wage to prevent poverty.

Even when there is work available, wages may be so low that a person or family cannot avoid poverty.

More common in Third World countries than in the developed world, conflict or civil war is a major cause of poverty among populations. Without the security provided by government, populations ensnared in conflict are unable to engage in consistent work necessary to avoid poverty. The civil war in Syria and ongoing conflicts in Latin America during the first part of the twenty-first century are emblematic of conditions which are conducive to poverty in these populations.

Racial, gender, and caste inequality in many countries also drive many into poverty. More common in Third World countries, systemic racism in the developed world, such as the United States, also prevents families from escaping the grip of poverty.

Another obvious cause of poverty is poor education. Again, while this is more common in Third World countries where girls are prohibited from attending school, it is seen also in many countries where the need to support families often prevents young families from getting the education necessary to avoid poverty. And where public education is available, facilities or teaching support is inadequate to provide the quality of education necessary to avoid poverty.

Sometimes overlooked among the causes of poverty is climate change. Especially in poor rural areas of many countries which depend on farming, drought and climactic events such as hurricanes and flooding often prevent families from earning their way out of poverty.

Another cause of poverty more common in undeveloped countries than in developed ones such as the United States is the lack of infrastructure. Many countries don't even have roads which small farmers can use to send their crops and produce to market.

Similarly, the lack of an electrical infrastructure prevents many families from earning a living which would keep them from poverty. And the inability to respond to natural disasters because of the lack of infrastructure means many families are driven to poverty simply because of the earthquakes, hurricanes, and tornadoes that would otherwise occur.

A more subtle, but nonetheless real, cause of poverty is the inequality which exists in different forms throughout the world. In India, for example, the existing caste system means that many of its citizens who are born into poverty are destined to remain there because of the caste in which they exist. But even in more developed nations inequality leads many to poverty. For example, the indigenous people of Australia have long been relegated to lesser positions in society, and to grinding endemic poverty, due to their origins, just as there are higher rates of poverty among African Americans and Native American Indians in the United States.

Another cause of poverty more common in some parts of the developed world is poor government. In countries such as Honduras, El Salvador, and Guatemala, thousands of their citizens flee to the north because their government cannot control the violence of criminal gangs or manage to provide economic growth and stability where all citizens benefit.

Finally, while it can be expected that populations among all nations periodically experience some or all these causes, most are able to bounce back using reserves built up in better times. But some nations, especially in some of the impoverished regions of the Middle East and sub-Saharan Africa, have never attained reserves to support them in times of need. Because of these inadequate reserves many of their populations continue to experience cycles of dire poverty due to any number of the causes just mentioned.

B. Income Inequality

Closely related to, and often the cause of, poverty, is *income inequality*. A very simple definition is the "growing gap between the wealthiest Americans and those struggling to get by on minimum wage."[4] But it is so much more than that. For one thing, the gap exists not only between the wealthiest Americans and those living on minimum wages, but between a large segment of the population who receive what many consider a just or a living wage and those receiving much lower wages. This inequality is often based on gender, race, socioeconomic class, or other divisions in society. For discussions about leadership and its potential effect on addressing income inequality, it (income inequality) can refer to any situation in which one group receives less than it should as a result of the classifications mentioned above (gender, race, socioeconomic class, or similar divisions in society). These disparities are generally subject to correction given the leadership of some person, government, or organization with the vision to see the problem and its implications clearly and the power to effect real change.

A well-known method of measuring income inequality uses the Lorentz Curve as shown in Figure 6-1.[5] The figure shows that the Lorenz Curve divides the area of the defined triangle into two areas A and B. At any point along the curve, say at 50 percent of people on the x axis, that point corresponds to the point on the y axis which indicates the share of income which that percentage of people earn, in this case (50 percent of the people) something a lot less than 50 percent of the income earned. Of course, the 100 percent point on the x axis, indicates that the entire population earns 100 percent of the income earned. The Line of Equality indicates that each percentage of population earns exactly that percentage of the total income earned.

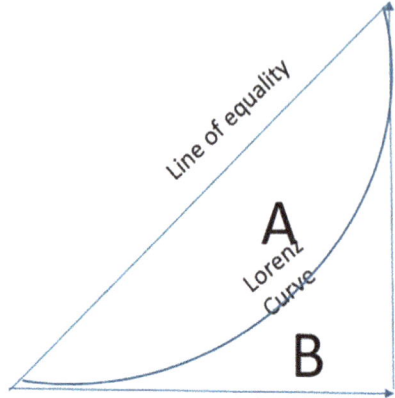

Figure 6-1.
The cumulative share of income vs cumulative share of people from lowest to highest income.

By inspection one sees that the closer the Lorenz curve comes to the Line of Equality, the share of income of all people approaches more closely the total income earned by all people at all levels. In other words, income equality increases to the point at which any segment of the population shares equally in the total earned. One way to describe this mathematically is through use of the expression $A/(A+B)$, termed the Gini coefficient, named after the Italian statistician. By inspection, the closer the Lorenz curve is to the Line of Equality, the smaller the ratio $A/(A+B)$, that is, the smaller the Gini coefficient, and the more equal is the income distribution in the population being considered. Approximate Gini coefficients for selected nations of the developed world are as follows.[6]

Denmark	0.25
Norway	0.27
Finland	0.28
Germany	0.29
Canada	0.32
France	0.33
United States	0.43
China	0.44
Peru	0.49
Chile	0.53
Brazil	0.55

Those nations in which there is a high degree of income equality (low Gini coefficient) include the Scandinavian countries, all of which have a Gini coefficient less than 0.3. Among the countries with the highest Gini coefficient—most unequal in income equality—are Peru, Chile, and Brazil. The United States has a coefficient of about 0.43.

The Gini coefficient provides in one number an indication of the degree of income inequality in a given country. According to some, however, this simplicity is also a negative in that, even using the Lorenz Curve in Figure 6-1, it is difficult to describe what income inequality is. Many prefer comparisons of income in the top 1 percent or 0.1 percent of a nation's population with the income in the bottom 90 percent or 50 percent.

The effects of income inequality are many. In the extreme among these is poverty, or not having the resources to provide the basic necessities of life, such as shelter and food. Another effect of income inequality is its effect on education. It's no wonder that elementary schools in more affluent districts have the best of facilities, and universities with healthy endowments supported by high-income alumni make such institutions of higher learning the envy of the world. And because many less fortunate members of society view income inequality as a matter of fairness (or lack thereof), and resent those who are more affluent, there is often a temptation to commit crime to correct this (the Robin Hood approach).

A more pervasive effect of income inequality on society is that on health. Not surprisingly, there is a strong correlation between income inequality and death rates, arising from many factors including access to quality health care. Many studies, including one in 2005 and published in the Journal of Epidemiology and Community Health, found that populations with higher Gini coefficients have shorter life expectancies, and infant mortality is higher among those who either can't afford decent pre-natal care or the attention that is more readily available to parents with higher incomes.

Not surprisingly, the incidence of mental illness is higher among people in countries with greater income inequality. In 2013 the International Journal of Social Psychiatry reported on a greater incidence of schizophrenia among those living in countries with greater income inequality.

With regard to infectious diseases, the Journal of the American Medical Association reported in 2021 that counties in the U.S. with higher Gini confidents (more income inequality) had a higher incidence of cases and deaths from COVID-19. Clearly, greater income inequality has a significant effect on health care among all populations.

Not as often discussed as an effect of income inequality is its effect on something called *social trust*, or the belief in, or confidence in, one's importance in society and one's willingness to participate in social conventions beneficial to all. When one's income is not only low, but clearly not reflective of his or her contribution to society, it is easy to feel not part of it, and even distrustful. This distrust often translates into the refusal to vote, follow accepted social conventions, and even to extend simply acts of kindness or courtesy to others.

For all these reasons, then, (increased poverty, reduced educational opportunities, increased crime, poor health care, and reduced social trust) it is not surprising that income inequality strongly influences a person's happiness. In general, populations with a high Geni coefficient tend to be less happy, probably out of a sense of fairness (or lack thereof), but also because of these many negative social impacts.

While there is evidence supporting the argument that income inequality actually supports economic growth, there is a greater case to be made that it hinders such growth. Confirming this, the International Monetary Fund reported in 2015 that economic growth is weaker in countries in which wealth is concentrated in the top 20 percent of the population.

With so many adverse effects of income inequality, the obvious question is what are its causes. Among these is the growth of technology throughout the developed world. With this growth has come the need for well-educated people to fill positions in business and industries which have become more dependent on technology and the latest scientific advances. This, in turn, has increased the importance of higher education and the competition for well-paying jobs which go to an already successful minority.

Related to this growth in technology is the globalization of businesses and industry, which has led to hiring the best and brightest throughout the world for high paying positions. Abetting this is the growth in immigration, which has led to both higher paying positions staffed by well-educated immigrants and much lower paying positions filled by immigrants fleeing Third World countries.

In the United States especially, the weakening of labor unions has led to a reduction of benefits and wages among organized workers, as evidenced by the fact that the federal minimum wage has not risen above $7.25 since 2009. With no pressure on management from organized labor to raise wages in so many industries, the inequity between highly paid persons and those earning just above the minimum wage will continue to grow.

At the other end of the spectrum is CEO compensation. CEO compensation has grown 940 percent since 1978, whereas that for workers has increased only 12 percent.[7] While this difference has declined somewhat since 2000, it's been consistently high since the 1990s compared to the years prior.

In a class of its own as to the effects on growing income inequality is the effect of government policies. Among these are tax cuts, probably best exemplified by the $1.5 trillion tax cut of 2017 which disproportionately benefited the wealthy over the middle and lower classes.

Similarly, deregulation and other government policies have made it more likely that business owners and the wealthier members of society benefit more financially than the lower and middle classes. In the same vein, weakened labor standards and social safety nets have benefited those with higher incomes more than those with lower incomes, contributing to the many ways government policies have increased income inequality.

Somewhat related to income inequality is wealth inequality. While the terms are closely related, wealth inequality does have a somewhat different meaning with significant implications. First, it's important to recognize that wealth is simply the difference between assets and liabilities, or the difference between what we have and what we owe to others; whereas income connotes a flow of money from some entity, say a job, position, or profession. Income inequality exists when income is less than what one might expect for reasons other than the nature of the work performed. Wealth inequality, on the other hand, might exist when the quantity of assets one possesses is less than one might have acquired were it not for reasons that he or she cannot control, among these possibly being race, gender, and inheritance (or lack thereof). In a sense, *wealth inequality is more significant in that wealth is actually a generator of income and* can magnify the extent of income inequality among a population.

Another major difference between income and wealth inequality is that the latter actually perpetuates inequality in society, as demonstrated by Thomas Piketty in his book *CAPITAL in the Twenty-First Century*.[8] Time and again, throughout the ages, wealth has begotten more wealth, with all that follows from it, often to the exclusion of others in society. Wealth, in itself, is not a bad thing, but if it disadvantages some members of society, it can be considered an undesirable thing.

II. Extent Internationally and the U.S.

One of the stark differences in the extent of poverty and income inequality throughout the world is the degree of each of these in developed and developing countries. Especially with regard to poverty, its existence in the Third World is so much more prevalent than almost anywhere in the developed world.

The reasons for the difference in poverty go back to modern economic development, especially since the Industrial Revolution beginning in the eighteenth century and extending to the current time. Most of the early technological innovations, such as the modern steam engine, had their beginnings in Great Britain, and they soon made their way to European nations – and the United States – which then used them to develop modern economies with active systems of trade with other developing nations. If the developing nations made their way to Africa, the Middle East, and Asia, it was usually to acquire their natural resources for use in the European (and American) economies. For many reasons, the governments of the resource providing nations failed to develop their own economies but served only to provide resources for wealthier nations.

While there are many reasons for this difference between developed and poorer nations, Jeffrey Sachs has identified in *The Age of Sustainable Development* several characteristics as factors leading to extreme poverty in many countries.[9] Among these is physical geography. While many cities in the United States are situated near large bodies of water which facilitated trade with other nations, such was not the case in many parts of the world, such as the interior of the African continent. Remote villages and cities there remained cut off from the more vibrant trade in the United States and Europe, and their populations suffered economically, even until the present day. The result is drastic poverty among much of their populations.

Another contributing factor for the extreme poverty among many of the world's developing nations is poor governance, specifically the lack of leadership in these countries. Especially in many nations of Central and South America, their leaders are rife with corruption, authoritarianism, or incompetence which restricts legitimate economic growth that would otherwise enable their populations to feed, house, and clothe themselves. Compounding this tragedy is the fact that many of the leaders in these countries and large corporations continue to enrich themselves at the expense of their population for whom assistance from NGOs and charities is intended.

A separate factor contributing to the poverty of many of the world populations—especially in the Middle East and South Asia—is cultural. In many nations girls and women are prohibited from participating in the same education and employment opportunities as boys and men. This, in turn, places an artificial drag on the economy, slowing its growth, and withholding financial security from much of their populations—particularly women.

Many nations such as India still employ caste systems in many of their regions, which consider large segments of their population unequal to other members of society and "unworthy" of sharing in society's economic benefits. This, of course, hinders the economic growth of entire nations, but it especially affects those members of the lower castes who often live their entire lives mired in poverty.

Another reason for which Third World or developing countries are distinguished by their poverty and income inequality among their populations is *geopolitics*. In some parts of the world, especially in the Middle East, but also in Asia and Latin America, certain countries are isolated or dominated by other more powerful nations and are kept from developing economically. Either as a result of foreign domination or civil war, these countries have failed to accumulate any degree of wealth or income comparable to the developed world. Consequently, while tracking in time with developed nations, especially during world crises, such as the financial crisis of 2007–2008, the degree of wealth and income inequality between developed and developing nations is significant.

One way to view the likely extent of poverty in underdeveloped nations is through the Human Development Index (HDI), a number between 0 and 1 which reflects a nation's development in education, life expectancy, and per capita income.[10] The lower a nation's HDI, the more likely it is that its population lives in poverty. As expected, the nations with the lowest HDIs are in sub-Saharan Africa and South Asia, and it can be expected that they are populated by most of the world's poor.

But there is a significant level of poverty – especially child poeverty – in developed nations, as can be seen in Figure 6-2 which shows its extent in devloped nations. Somewhat surprising is the fact that only Chile and Turkey have higher levels of child poverty than the United States.

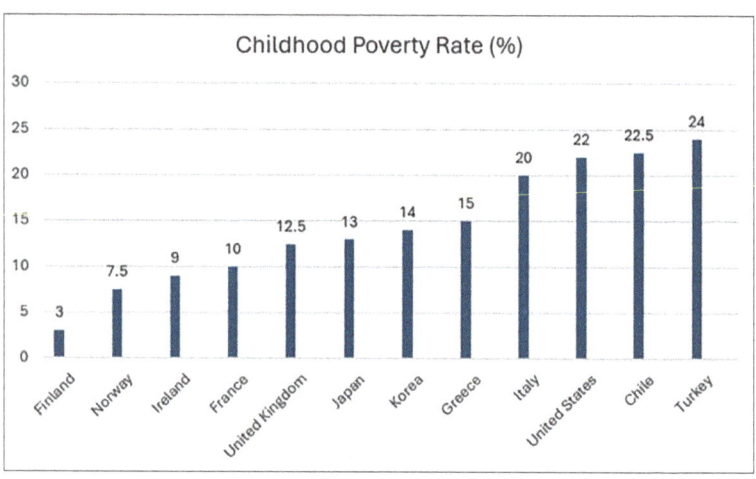

Figure 6-2.
Childhood poverty rate among developed nations. Source:
National Center for Biotechnology Information

Income inequality can be viewed from two different perspectives – the inequality between developed nations and developing nations, and that within nations (usually developed ones). With regard to the difference between developed and developing nations, in 1975 the national income of developed nations was ten times greater than that of developing nations.[11] Some forty years later this global income inequality has fortunately decreased.

Poverty and Income Inequality

Unfortunately, the same cannot be said about equality among nations of the developed world, especially the United States. While middle-income levels have increased somewhat, those of higher income levels have increased much more. What's more, the aggregate lower-income percentage of total national income has actually decreased, as shown in Figure 6-3, again as reported by the Pew Research Center. Whereas, in 1970 the percentage of national aggregate income attributed to middle income was 62 percent, and that attributed to upper income was 29 percent, by 2018 the percentages were actually reversed. The percentage of aggregate national income which was considered middle income declined to 43 percent, and the percentage which was considered upper income increased to 48 percent. The percentage of aggregate income which was considered lower actually declined from 10 percent to 9 percent. But, as noted earlier, race is an aggregator of poverty in that being Black or Hispanic increases the likelihood of living in poverty.

Figure 6-3
Incomes for Upper-, Middle-, and Low-Income Levels.
Pew Research Center Trends in income and wealth inequality

The reasons for this are primarily two. Throughout the latter part of the twentieth century, global trade has increased dramatically, largely because of lower labor costs, which have reduced the income of middle- and lower-income groups. At the same time, upper income groups benefited from this same reduction in labor costs, resulting in their increased income at the same time middle- and lower-income groups were seeing their wages reduced due to increased exports. Population growth slowed significantly also, resulting in the loss of reduced economic growth and aggregate income among the middle- and lower-income groups. The result is an increase in income inequality in the U.S. and probably in other developed nations for the same reason.

III. Sustainable Development Impact

A. Poverty

Poverty's effect on sustainable development is, perhaps, most noticeable, in its effect on the environment.[12] In many parts of the world, deforestation is the only way many of the poor can clear enough land to grow just subsistence crops for their families. But removing trees and other vegetation to clear the land for farming also reduces an important global sink for carbon dioxide and increases the accumulation of greenhouse gases in the atmosphere. Such destruction of forests in the Amazon, for instance, also leads to habitat destruction and the loss of endangered species, as well as the loss of exotic plant, animals, and aquatic and marine life which could have research and medicinal value.

Poverty brings with it significant economic costs.[13] Among these are those associated with child poverty including reduced earnings, increased victimization costs of street crime, increased health costs, and increased corrections and crime prevention costs. These are the major increased costs, but there are additional costs as well, with the total accounting for over a trillion dollars per year, which accounts for over 5 percent of the U.S. Gross Domestic Product. Certainly, from both an economic standpoint and just from childhood poverty, this is not sustainable.

There are social equity effects of poverty also. Possibly the most indicative of sustainable development impacts is the health of an individual. In one study close to a quarter of Coloradans living in poverty have fair or poor health compared with only 9.6 percent of those not in poverty.[14] Probably related is the fact that those not in poverty live six to ten years longer than those who are, and children who live in poverty are more likely to be depressed than those who don't.

And there are less tangible effects of poverty on social equity.[15] Among these is the fact that those living in poverty have a lower sense of dignity and self-worth than those who are not impoverished. As a result, many of those living in poverty will often not claim benefits to which they are entitled out of shame for their condition. Because many activities of social interaction require money, those living in poverty will avoid interacting with others. Finally, out of shame for their condition, people living in poverty will often deny that they are poor, and thus they are unwilling to avail themselves of assistance from others wanting to help them.

B. Income Inequality

The effects of income inequality on sustainable development are similar to the effects of poverty, especially at lower income levels–although not nearly as drastic. What is significant is the fact that income inequality is growing in the United States, and it is higher in America than almost any other developed country.[16] It's growth in the U.S., as measured by Gini coefficient, has increased steadily over the last seventy-five years.

In addition to the effects of poverty on sustainable development, the effects of income inequality, especially given its acceleration over the last seventy-five years, are particularly harmful to the economic development of the nation as a whole. For sustained economic growth, in which all members of society share in the benefits of that growth, everyone should feel they are part of it, and have a stake in its success.

As emphasized in Thomas Piketty's book, *CAPITAL in the Twenty-First Century*, income inequality, especially when increasing, perpetuates the accumulation of wealth among families. This, in turn, provides better health care, access to more and better education, and, in general, more opportunities for select groups of individuals based on wealth. Such conditions run counter to all that is assumed in the sustainable development of democracies.

IV. Leadership Opportunities to Address Poverty and Income Inequality

A. Government

Most of the opportunities to address poverty and income inequality are challenging and far reaching enough to require the resources of, and enforcement by, government. And their criticality and potential impact on sustainable development are of such magnitude that they are more than worthy of pursuit. Among these governmental opportunities to address poverty and income inequality are a transparent and democratic trade policy, the prevention of illegal financial flows, steps to ensure a living wage, a more progressive tax policy, and stronger unions.[17]

The first of these—a transparent and democratic trade policy—would ensure that trade decisions are not based only on the cheaper labor costs in foreign countries. When companies such as Walmart make low prices for consumer goods a priority by purchasing them offshore where labor is cheapest, domestic labor wages are driven downward. At the same time the profits of major corporations rise with those running them seeing their income increase, thus aggravating national income inequality. Such practices—increasing the import of cheaper foreign goods leading to more income inequality—are a function of trade policy and can be managed by the federal government.

Another way to minimize poverty and income inequality is to reduce illegal—and often legal—financial outflows from the country. Such outflows increase the concentration of wealth—and income—of the higher income brackets of the country, often at the expense of lower ones. In the extreme, the impact on sustainable development is the fact that resources that could be used to address issues of concern that affect the entire population of a nation, such as homelessness and hunger, remain in the hands of a relative few. Tax avoidance, in which large companies incorporate in usually smaller countries with a much lower tax structure, is probably the most common example. But, as revealed by the International Consortium of Investigative Journalists in mid-2012, the Pandora Papers, consisting of 11.9 million files describing efforts to conceal the financial assets of extremely wealthy investors, the problem is much greater than previously thought.[18] To make matters even worse, these investors included at least 331 government officials, including 35 world leaders whose responsibilities ostensibly included the financial integrity of their governments.

The current federal minimum wage is $7.25, which took effect in 2009, and this equates to less than $15,000 per year—hardly enough to support an individual, let alone a family, though it is within the power of government to mandate through the Fair Labor Standards Act raising the minimum wage for covered jobs and positions. Given the length of time since it was raised, families depending now on the federal minimum wage can hardly provide themselves the necessities of life. Increasing its level now would enable more people to avail themselves of better shelter, nutrition, education, and the other necessities of sustainable development.

While the tax structure in the United States is currently progressive, more can be done to better reflect the returns large corporations and high-income wealthy individuals receive for the taxes they pay, vis a vis lower-income individuals; in other words, make the tax system more progressive. An argument can be made that wealthy individuals receive much more for their taxes in terms of personal and national security, and physical infrastructure conducive to business success, than lower-income individuals and businesses. So, how can one justify some large corporations and individuals paying effectively no taxes on their income and wealth?

Finally, another contributor to income and wealth inequality is the decline in union membership in the United States. In 1979, 34 percent of American workers belonged to unions, while in 2016 union membership declined to 10 percent. Without the ability to demand higher wages and better working conditions, workers must settle for incomes which exacerbate income inequality in the nation. But government, primarily through legislation such as the Fair Labor Standards Act, can institute changes which will ensure higher incomes for lower- and middle-income workers.

B. Businesses and Organizations

Businesses affect income inequality in three ways: corruption, scalability, and undervalued resources.[19] The first two of these, corruption and scalability, increase income inequality, whereas the third, undervalued resources, tends to reduce income inequality.

With regard to corruption, this is probably one of the most evident causes of inequality, since, by definition, it involves actions by large corporations to do (or not do) things that, while financially attractive, are harmful to the public. Consider the practice several years ago of a major automobile manufacturer which adjusted its engine operation to indicate a lower degree of emissions than it (the manufacturer) knew existed. This practice probably increased sales of its vehicles, leading to increased income for its investors with no financial benefit to its customers. The result is an increase in income inequality. Numerous other examples exist, in which businesses increase their income through corrupt, or at least, questionable, business practices.

Another way income inequality increases is through scalability. If any new product, technology, or innovation is very successful throughout the economy, it is said to *scale,* or increase in growth with consequent large financial gains or income to the originator or developer, but not necessarily to those using the product or innovation. The result is an increase in income inequality. Examples in the current economy are Google, Apple, Tesla, and many others. Incidentally, even though there is an increase in income inequality, the new product, technology, or innovation is probably good for the economy as a whole.

The final example of how businesses affect income inequality, and actually reduce it, is through *undervalued resources.* The best example of this may be the availability of cheap labor in Japan after

World War II and in China throughout most of the twentieth century. With the availability of cheap labor in East Asia, western nations took advantage of this previously undervalued resource (inexpensive labor) to increase their import of products from Japan, China, Malaysia, and several other nations in this region. The result was increased demand for products from the Far East, and an increase in the wages for workers of these nations, resulting in a reduction in income inequality.

Regardless of the way in which businesses affect income inequality, it should be evident that leadership plays a significant role setting in motion the conditions which, do, in fact affect income inequality. In the case of corruption in a business, such corruption is obviously the result of corrupt decisions by its leaders—or at least the refusal of its leaders to do the right thing—an attribute of leadership. In the case of scalability, it's often the vision of leaders in a business which enables its leaders to develop a product or technology which scales to such an extent that the leaders' incomes increase proportionately to the success of the product or technology. Of course, the users of the products or technology also benefit financially, but not generally to the same extent as those responsible (the leaders) for the product or technology. Finally, in the case of taking advantage of undervalued resources, it's again the leaders' vision which discerns the potential benefit of using these resources.

C. Individuals

The opportunities for individual leadership in addressing the challenges of income inequality exist foremost in government and business, because the policies established by government, and the societal effects of the operations of businesses are the result only of the goals of the people implementing them. One might consider the leadership of President Franklin Roosevelt between 1933 and 1939 in developing and implementing the New Deal which completely transformed the income structure of the low and middle classes for generations. Or consider President Lyndon Johnson and his Great Society in 1964–1965 whose legislative achievements had a similar effect on American workers and their incomes and their part in the American dream.

Individuals may find opportunities to address income inequality through advocacy. This may take many forms, but possibly the most visible, and effective, is through organizing and participating in public protests and rallies to promote legislation and call for regulatory changes to advance income equality and by advocating for such causes as an increased minimum wage, more progressive tax measures, and increased benefits for caregivers. Individuals can also demonstrate leadership by writing letters to their state representatives and their members of congress advocating for such measures. Or one can write letters to the editor in one's local or national newspapers. All these opportunities to demonstrate personal leadership in advancing the cause of income equality are open to individuals who are committed to the cause of sustainable equity.

V. Examples of Leadership in Addressing Income Inequality

A. Government

In addition to the New Deal and Great Society programs already mentioned, numerous other government programs and policies have advanced the struggle to address income inequality. One of the most effective of these government programs was the Civilian Conservation Corps (CCC), established in 1933 as part of Franklin Roosevelt's New Deal. The purpose of the CCC was to provide work relief, and much needed income, to thousands of unemployed Americans at the height of the Great Depression. Before it was abolished, the CCC was responsible for planting three billion trees and developing 800 parks and trails throughout the country. In just a few months the CCC was able to provide jobs and income to over 300,000 Americans, which directly influenced income inequality throughout the country at a time when the need was most critical.

Another example of government leadership in addressing income inequality was construction of the Interstate Highway System, which began with the *Federal Highway Act of 1956* under President Dwight D. Eisenhower. Not only did development of the highway system provide employment and income to tens of thousands of Americans for years to come, but it was influential in the post-World War II economic growth of the country.

B. Business and Organizations—Economic Policy Institute

The Economic Policy Institute (EPI) is a nonprofit, nonpartisan think tank created in 1986 to include the needs of low- and middle-income workers in economic policy discussions.[20] Its goal is to put forth and advocate for policies that ensure that workers share in the economic success of the nation. While its goal is to assist all workers in this effort, a large part of it is to assist people of color and indigenous people. One of its major achievements was its publishing *State of Working America in 1988*, which has been published twelve times since. Considered the authority on the subject, the book is used by universities throughout the world in teaching the subject of working conditions and compensation.

EPI is also well-known for illustrating and popularizing the decoupling of productivity and worker pay. Until the latter part of the twentieth century worker compensation followed closely with the rise in the economic success and productivity of the nation, but since then, there's been a divergence (decoupling) in worker compensation and productivity. This is shown in Figure 6-4, which tracks the growth of these two variables over the twentieth century. EPI has been instrumental in revealing and publicizing this disparity and has influenced measures to reduce it.

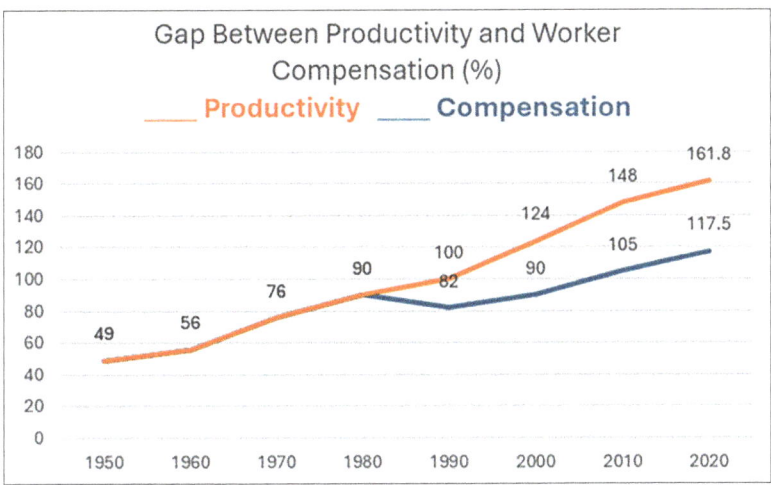

Figure 6-4
Gap between productivity and worker compensation. Source: Economic Policy Institute

Obviously, workers' wages increased with growth in the economy until the mid-1970s when they diverged significantly until the period 1979-2020, and during this period, while the economy grew by 61.8 percent, worker compensation grew only by 17.5 percent. There are probably many reasons for this, but one of the most significant would be the reduced participation in union membership during this period. Without a strong voice among the lower and middle class, worker compensation among these groups will continue to lag that of more highly compensated groups.

Among the most noteworthy accomplishments of EPI was its role in forming the Economic Analysis and Research Network (EARN). This organization is a group of state and regional research units with similar goals, especially as regards lower-income workers. By combining the resources of all such research units, EARN can be more effective in reducing income inequality in society, and EPI has provided the leadership in achieving its goals.

C. Individual—Senator Bernie Sanders

Senator Bernie Sanders is an excellent example of an individual who has displayed leadership in addressing income inequality. Even though he has held numerous positions in government, his accomplishments reflect not policies or legislation, but his tireless advocacy for working people and their achieving income equality with upper-income persons. Growing up in Flatbush in Brooklyn, New York, he knew from an early age what it meant to be poor and his awareness of the income disparity between the "haves" and "have nots" never left him.

Beginning as the Mayor of Burlington, Vermont, and then during successive stints in the U.S. House of Representatives and Senate, the urgent need to address the issue of income inequality has always been his distinguishing belief. Perhaps one of the public discourses for which he is best known is *The Speech: A Historic Filibuster on Corporate Greed and the Decline of Our Middle Class* (2011), reflecting his belief in the disparity in compensation of the middle and upper classes. And during both runs for the Presidency in 2016 and 2020 in which he proudly declared himself a social democrat, Senator Sanders distinguished himself from the other candidates by his position on income inequality. Perhaps no other person in public life has shown as much leadership in speaking out for the worker in America.

References

1. Sam Okalow, *What is poverty? It's not as simple as you think*, May 20, 2021, World Vision.
2. Maryann Broxton, Guillaume Charvon, and Dave Meyer, *Pushed to the Bottom the Experience of Poverty in the United States*, 2019, ATD.
3. Kristin Myers, *The top 9 causes of global* poverty, May 3, 2018, UN Office for the Coordination of Human Affairs.
4. Amy Livingston, *Income Inequality in America – Definitions, Causes & Statistics*, June 11, 2021, Money Crashers.
5. Matthew Yglesias, *Everything you need to know about income inequality*, May 12, 2015, Vox.
6. Yglesias, *Everything you need . . ..*
7. Lawrence Mishel and Julia Wolfe, *CEO compensation has grown 940% since 1978*, August 14, 2019, Economic Policy Institute.
8. Thomas Piketty, *CAPITAL in the Twenty-First Century*, 2014, Cambridge, Massachusetts.
9. Jeffrey Sachs, *The Age of Sustainable Development*, 2015, Columbia University Press.
10. Max Roser, *Human Development Index (HDI)*, Our World in Data, November, 2019.
11. Norwich University Online, *Global Economic Inequality–and What Might Be Done About*. October 6, 2020.
12. Chante Owens, *How Poverty Impacts the Environment*, October 2, 2013, The Borgen Project.
13. *What Are the Economic Costs of Child Poverty?* April 21, 2021, Peter G. Peterson Foundation.

14. centerforhealth, *LIFE AT THE FEDERAL POVERTY LEVEL*, CENTER FOR HEALTH PROGRESS, March 8, 2018.
15. *Understanding social work and poverty*, British Association of Social Workers.
16. *A Guide to Economic Inequality*, April 2021, American Compass.
17. Norwich University, *Global Economic Inequality*.
18. Dean Starkman et al, *Frequently asked questions about the Pandora Papers and ICIJ*, October 19, 2021, International Consortium of Investigative Journalists.
19. Bill Conerly, *Business Is One Reason for Economic Inequality—And Also For Equality*, Sept. 23, 2018, Forbes.
20. ww.epi.org.

7

Social and Environmental Justice

I. Definitions and Background

A. Social Justice

The United Nations has defined in very general terms social justice as, "Social justice may be broadly understood as the fair and compassionate distribution of the fruits of economic growth."[1] And the National Association of Social Workers has expanded this definition with the statements "Social justice is the view that everyone deserves equal economic, political, and social rights and opportunities. Social workers aim to open the doors of access and opportunities for everyone, particularly those in greatest need."[2] This expansion adds to the UN definition by including political and social rights in addition to economic benefit, and thus implies the concern for how we treat people as human beings. Moreover, it addresses the need for "access and opportunities" as rights of these human beings. In other words, everyone deserves to have the same chance to improve their lives simply because they are human.

There are many versions of principles of social justice, but one of the most common versions is that especially pertinent to public administration listed by Kent State University.[3] These principles of social justice are Access, Equity, Diversity, Participation, and Human Rights.

By *Access* is meant equal availability to everyone of resources normally accorded to all members of society. Public education is an excellent example of a just system since the availability of education in large part determines an individual's future. But other examples exist, such as health care, employment opportunities, and economic advancement.

Another principle of social justice is *Equity*, by which is meant treating people with a view to their needs as defined by some commonly accepted standard. For example, is it fair to include on college admission tests questions that one could reasonably expect only those from a certain socioeconomic class to be able to answer? Or is it fair to restrict entry for disabled persons to otherwise public venues? In this context another word for equity might be *fairness*.

A related principle of social justice would be *Diversity*, which recognizes the differences among human beings with regard to gender, sexual orientation, religion, age, marital status, and similar attributes of nature or personal choice. A distinguishing feature of these traits is that they have no outward, physical adverse effect on others by their existence.

Somewhat related to the previously mentioned Access is *Participation*. Simply stated, this means that everyone has a right to be heard in decisions affecting them. Probably the best example of this is voting in a democratic society. Often taken for granted, especially in the United States, the right to vote is the outward sign of self-determination, or the ability for everyone to have a say in what affects them and their lives. Major accomplishments in social justice are marked in our own history by women and African Americans achieving the right to vote. But there are other less obvious examples of the right of participation in our society such as public demonstrations, speaking before elected political bodies, and even writing letters to the editor in the local newspaper.

Perhaps the most important of the principles of social justice is *Human Rights*, which are so important because they all extend from the simple but most basic condition of our existence. In other words, simply because we are human, we have a right to believe—or not believe—in a Creator, the right not to be held against our will, the right not to be physically harmed, the right of personal privacy, and any number of rights, simply because we are human. Reflecting this importance is the fact that the United Nations has a special body—the United Nations Human Rights Council—which monitors and addresses the observance of human rights throughout the world.

Such are the building blocks, if you will, of social justice. These are the foundation of how we should treat each other in addressing so many issues in society. Some of these are as follows.

A direct consequence of the diminished Access seen by many experiencing social injustice is the lack of *Affordable Health Care*. Predominantly in the United States among developed nations, affordable health care is limited to either the very wealthy, or those fortunate to work for companies that subsidize and provide it. Unfortunately, those without health care comprise about 8.5 percent, or 27.5 million of the American population, according to the most recently available census figures.[5] This, in turn, results in the most harmful effects on those without medical care, including personal bankruptcies of those unable to pay for it, or, in the worst cases, illness or even death for those who are forced by finances to go without care.

A somewhat surprising potential social injustice is that caused by *Climate Change*. By now it's well-known that those most affected by the adverse effects of climate change are the poor and marginalized of the world. This is evident in the threat from rising sea levels in many of the low-lying communities of Pacific Islands and the coastal communities of poorer nations such as Bangladesh. Also, water scarcity stemming from climate change induced drought usually affects those communities unable to find alternate sources of supply. Poorer populations without expensive air conditioning will be the most affected by rising temperatures caused by climate change.

Related to Climate Change is *Food Insecurity and Hunger*, which often affects those least able to afford adequate nutrition. Often brought on by the loss of crops due to drought and other effects of climate change, there are other causes of food insecurity tied to social injustice. One of these is the prevalence of "food deserts" in lower socioeconomic areas, caused by the reluctance of major supermarket chains to locate in such areas. Whatever the reason, there is a scarcity of fresh fruits and vegetables in these areas not seen in more affluent areas. Another cause is the relative expense of healthier foods, an expense that lower-income shoppers often choose not to bear, especially when cheaper, processed, or "junk" foods are available. In any case, the result is food insecurity and hunger that is simply not seen in higher-income groups.

As already discussed earlier under income inequality, there is a stark *Income Gap* between the "haves" and "have nots." While such inequality is often the result of economic factors and structure, there are also issues of social injustice that contribute to this intractable problem. For example, many of those in higher-income groups have been fortunate to attend the best (and most expensive) schools. But sadly, access to higher-income employment is often differentiated by race and gender.

Some of the most direct issues associated with violation of the principles of social justice are those having to do with *LGBTQ+* (Lesbian, Gay, Bi-sexual, Transgender, Queer) rights. While issues of race, gender, and religion are often protected by the Constitution and government regulations, issues of sexuality are not always so readily accepted in society. Yet such issues are as much a part of one's identity as race and gender, and thus they are to be considered part of one's identity as a human being, and as such, they constitute issues of social justice.

But the importance of racial equality should not be underestimated. Arguably, there is probably no other issue of social injustice which has so permeated American society as this, which should be no surprise. It doesn't take the notoriety of *The 1619 Project* or the high-energy public debate (warranted or not) about Critical Race Theory to see the prevailing influence of racism in our country. The emphasis here is, indeed, "in our country" as the United States is unique in this issue of social justice among developed nations. Certainly, there is racism throughout the world, but nowhere is there the systematic, structural racism, often hidden in legalisms, as there has been in the United States throughout its history and today. Consider the practice of "red lining," in which African Americans were prohibited from living in certain neighborhoods – a practice which existed well into the twentieth century. Or consider the overwhelming incidence of COVID infections, hospitalizations, and deaths among people of color (POC) compared to Caucasians. These are only two of the many examples of structural racism which have existed (and often still exist) in the United States

Finally, the one issue of social justice which can have an influence on achieving justice in all these areas is the issue of Voting Rights, for it is only when members of society have a role in determining what rights they do or do not have can they be assured that they will have those rights. Unfortunately, too often members of society underestimate their ability to effect change by exercising their right to vote. While each member of society does, in fact, have only their vote to effect change, they can do all in their power to influence others to vote. If each person can influence ten others to vote, and each of those ten others can influence ten others to vote, and so on, real change can result from the exercise of voting rights.

B. Environmental Justice

According to the United States Environmental Protection Agency (EPA), Environmental Justice "is the fair treatment and meaningful involvement of all people regardless of race, color, national origin, or income with respect to the development, implementation and enforcement of environmental laws, regulations, and policies."[6] Key to this definition is the manner in which society and government treat all people, regardless of their distinguishing characteristics, such as race or national origin, in matters which affect them, such as laws, policies, and regulations. Implied also is the necessity that all people participate in these matters, regardless of their distinguishing characteristics.

At the First National People of Color Environmental Leadership Summit, October 24–27, 1991, in Washington, D.C., delegates agreed on 17 Principles of Environmental Justice, which have since become the standard for the environmental justice movement.[7] Among these, several particularly reflect the urgency of this movement.

One of these is the demand that public policy decisions be made without partiality or prejudice to anyone due to race, religion, or country of origin as noted in the definition of environmental justice. This very general mandate says simply that issues of governance, public regulation, and just the way people are treated should be made with fairness to everyone regardless of who they are. This implies that everyone affected by such policy decisions be afforded the opportunity to participle at every level of planning, discussion, and decision-making.

Another principle is more specific in that it calls for the end of production of toxic materials, hazardous wastes, radioactive substances, and similar harmful materials, and containment of those already existing from harming people. Furthermore, it calls for holding those producing such materials accountable for detoxifying them at the point of production and not just where they are causing harm. The implication, of course, is the fact that points of production and ultimate dispersal are often in areas disproportionately populated by people of color or people of lower socioeconomic status.

Implied also is the fact all workers are entitled to a safe and healthy workplace. Workers should not have to decide between keeping their jobs and maintaining their health and safety. There are numerous instances of corporations, in an effort to cut costs and improve profit margins opt to cut corners, but these efforts endanger employees by permitting an unsafe working environment. Unfortunately, lower-income workers often pay the price with threats to their health and safety.

One way to ensure these principles of environmental justice achieve prominence in society and the workplace is through education and training. Both today and in the future, by ensuring these principles become part of organized education in high schools and universities, it becomes more likely that they will be realized in society and the workplace. Related to this, consumers can do their part by choosing to patronize businesses and corporations which practice environmental justice. When these businesses and corporations begin to see their adherence to the principles of environmental justice reflected in the bottom line (or not), they will adjust their operations to more closely follow them.

Just as there are numerous examples which illustrate the lack of social justice in society, there are also those which show shortcomings in environmental justice.

In September of 1982, 6,000 truckloads of toxic waste including polychlorinated biphenyls (PCBs) made their way to Afton, a small rural community of mostly African Americans in Warren County, North Carolina.[8] Residents of the community began six weeks of protests largely in fear of the PCBs leaking into the local water supply, during which 500 protesters were arrested. Even though the protests were unsuccessful, and the toxic waste was placed in the landfill, they drew national attention and the event is generally considered to be the beginning of the environmental justice movement.

Another case of environmental injustice occurred, and affects farmworkers, in the San Joaquin Valley of California. Much of the nation's produce is grown in California, and 88 percent of the farmworkers are Latino.[9] According to The Centers for Disease Control and Prevention, agriculture is one of the most hazardous industries with regard to human health.[10] The working environment is especially hazardous, given the toxic fertilizers and pesticides used to grow fruits and vegetables, and harvesting presents backbreaking work that only predominantly immigrants from Mexico will do. Due to the runoff from these hazardous chemicals into groundwater, the water ingested by these workers is harmful to their health, and medical care is sporadic due, among other things, to the seasonal nature of the work. To make matters even worse, for many reasons, the workers have little or no government representation to address the conditions under which they work.

While there are many other conditions of environmental injustice both internationally and in the United States, perhaps one of the best known and most serious is the one that occurred in Flint, Michigan, in 2014.[11] By then, Flint's population was predominantly African American due to the decline of the auto industry in the 1980s. As a cost-saving measure the city had decided to shift its water supply from the City of Detroit to the Flint River, even though the river had long been a disposal site for toxic materials from many of the industrial companies along its length. When service began to the older homes of Flint, many of which still had the original lead pipes, the toxic water leached harmful lead from these pipes into the water supplied to the homes.

Soon there occurred numerous cases of skin rash, hair loss, and elevated blood lead levels among the residents. These elevated levels of lead in the blood of children were especially frightening, as it has long been known that any incidence of lead in children affected their neurological development with lifelong effects. There was also an outbreak of Legionnaires disease from which twelve people died between June of 2014 and October of 2015.

It wasn't until the fall of 2015 when test results showing elevated levels of lead in drinking water that local citizens joined the National Resources Defense Council (NRDC) in petitioning the Environmental Protection Agency to take action. Unfortunately, the EPA didn't follow through, and a local group of citizens, Concerned Pastors for Social Action, the ACLU, and NRDC, sued the City of Flint in early 2016 to have all water tested and treated for lead and replace all lead pipes. In November a federal judge decided in the plaintiffs' favor, and all homes were to be provided bottled water and have a water filter installed. Even more important, it was decided the following spring to have all lead pipes serving homes in the city replaced.

While the final outcome of the Flint water crisis was favorable, there was literally untold damage done to the residents of Flint, especially to the children, due to this violation of environmental justice. If the city of Flint were populated by more affluent, whiter citizens, it is doubtful that the switch from Detroit's water supply to the Flint River would have occurred, nor would the eventual lead poisoning of the water have taken so long to correct.

C. Interconnectedness of Social and Environmental Justice

The prevailing attitudes about social and environmental justice often suffer from several harmful assumptions. For one thing, many people often consider the earth (nature) to be separate from humanity, and therefore exploitable. After all, whom does it hurt to despoil our atmosphere, rivers, oceans, and plant life? If they are not human, how is anybody hurt by harming or even destroying them? What difference does it make for various species to go extinct if the human species can continue?

On the contrary, damage to the environment does, in fact, harm human beings. By polluting the atmosphere, we harm those who breathe the air we breathe. By poisoning water supplies with industrial waste runoff, we sicken or even kill those human beings who drink that water. By destroying marine life, we make it more difficult for those who depend on it for food.

Another harmful assumption concerning social and environmental justice is the belief by many, especially those in developed countries, that the people in developing countries are exploitable. How else can we explain the practice of developed countries sending their often-hazardous waste to developing countries for disposal, knowing that it (the waste) will often be exposed to children who will pick through it for valuables? Or why is it okay for large corporations to employ poor indigenous people of the Amazon in mining copper under harmful environmental conditions? Even in the United States it was at one time considered acceptable to own slaves to extract profit from the environment. The answer to all these questions is the fact that developed nations often considered it perfectly acceptable to exploit other human beings, which is the epitome of social injustice.

An additional harmful aspect of the relationship between social and environmental justice is the fact that climate change often affects marginalized populations more than it does more affluent, successful ones. The reasons for this include the fact that marginalized people are often not able to mitigate the effects of climate change such as finding alternate sources of water or compensating for crop shortages caused by desertification. Or they are more dependent for their livelihood on pursuits such as agriculture or fishing that are disproportionately affected by climate change.

Another way in which climate change has a greater impact on poor or marginalized people is the fact that natural disasters such as flooding from hurricanes and wildfires from drought are more likely to occur in places in which they live. For example, consider the people of the Marshall Islands or Bangladesh who will be disproportionately affected by rising sea levels because they have no choice as to where they live.

The intersection of social and environmental justice is again illustrated in developed nations in which wealthy corporations operate businesses harmful to the environment and are able to hire only those who desperately need jobs. The agricultural industry has already been mentioned, but there are others. For example, the coal mines of West Virginia and Kentucky not only facilitate the continued use of coal to produce energy, which emits climate warming emissions, ruins otherwise pristine landscapes in those states, and poisons the drinking water in the process. While this is occurring, the corporations continue production which results in miners often contracting black lung disease, the treatment of which these corporations try to avoid.

Finally, many large corporations outsource mining and other operations to foreign countries where they can avoid strict environmental oversight in the United States and take advantage of cheaper labor in these countries. These same poorly paid workers often live near the hazardous waste sites created by these operations and drink ground water poisoned in the process.

The best example of social and environmental injustice would have to be climate change. In this instance, one party – usually developed countries with industries that emit greenhouse gases (GHGs) – enjoys the economic benefit without paying externalized costs. At the same time, the rest of the world—often developing countries without heavily emitting industries—pays the price of such emissions with rising sea levels, air pollution, desertification, and other adverse effects of climate change, without enjoying the economic benefits.

But even if these developing countries simply experienced the adverse effects of climate change without having to pay the costs, it is doubly unjust because those experiencing these adverse effects are often the poor and marginalized citizens of these countries. This is because the poor are usually without the resources to move inland if they are living along the coasts, or they find work in industries that are especially harmed by climate change, such as agriculture. Or they are dependent on marine life for their food, which is diminished due to the acidification of the ocean from CO_2 buildup from emitted GHGs.

Another excellent example of environmental injustice is the case in which polluting industries locate next to lower socioeconomic communities. These industries do this because the residents in these communities are, for several reasons, not politically involved, and generally, will not vigorously oppose their presence. Perhaps they are not aware that they can oppose the industries being there. Or, perhaps they are undocumented and hesitant to bring attention to themselves. In any case, they suffer the consequences of toxic waste, polluted air, or poisoned water simply because the polluting industries can take advantage of the communities' not speaking up, which is the height of social injustice.

II. Extent Internationally and in the U.S.

A. Differences Internationally and in the United States

There is a marked difference in the extent of social and environmental injustice internationally and in the United States. Internationally, this injustice often stems from cultural differences within nations. Consider the caste system in India, in which certain groups of people are deemed less worthy of respect than others, simply because they were born into a lower caste. Or consider the role of women in many Middle Eastern countries, where women cannot engage in activities outside the home without male accompaniment. And then there are the countries in which large groups of indigenous people who were often the first to settle there, such as the Aborigines in Australia or Native Americans in the United States, receive less respect than the rest of the population.

Related to these causes of social and environmental injustice are those cases in which large corporations take advantage of indigenous populations by subjecting them to hazardous working conditions or paying them pitifully low wages because they can get away with it. This is often the case in the Amazon where native habitat is destroyed to gain access to natural resources. Or consider copper mines in Africa which employ local workers at low wages in dangerous working conditions.

In the United States instances of social and environmental injustice often stem from its history of slavery in which African Americans were treated as less than human, or, at most, "three-fifths" of a free person. While slavery no longer exists in the U.S., the vestiges of such treatment do still exist in many parts of the country, such as the practice of "Redlining" which has existed in many zoning laws. And related to this is the country's history of immigration in which large numbers of immigrants settled in the United States. For various reasons, these immigrants were either unwilling, or unable, to oppose blatant acts of discrimination and were thus victims of social injustice.

Also contributing to social and environmental injustice is the economic system in this country, in which lower socioeconomic groups tend to live in parts of the country more subject to environmental or developmental degradation. For example, housing developments near refineries in Houston or Long Beach have a much higher incidence of cancer and other diseases due to their proximity to the pollution from these facilities.[12] And, due to the undesirability of developments near the refineries, they are often populated by African Americans, Latinos, and other people of color, who are disproportionately affected by the pollution from these facilities.

B. International Extent

As noted, the incidence of environmental and social injustice differs somewhat among developed and undeveloped, or Third World countries. This difference is most evident from the work of the Environmental Justice Atlas, which tracks the extent of such injustice throughout the world.[13] According to this authority the ten most common types and number of such injustices (conflicts), as of 2018, are shown below.

- Land grabbing conflicts (600)

- Renewable energy (31 wind and 326 water infrastructure)

- Mega-mining (270)

- Unburnable fuels (178)

- Trash (126)

- Sand mafias (82)

- Fighting for fish (77)

- China rising up (76)

- Nuclear nightmares (57)

- Pesticide use (23)

Also as noted earlier, the predominance of such environmental injustice is in the Third World nations of South America and South Asia, even though they occur also in North America and Europe.

C. American Extent

Among the instances of environmental injustice in the United States are those cases where people of color live in areas disproportionately affected by pollution or toxic waste. According to the Proceedings of the National Academy of Sciences (March, 2019), Latinx Americans are exposed to 63 percent more pollution than they produce, and black Americans are exposed to 56 percent more. Contrast this to white Americans who are exposed to 17 percent less pollution than they produce.

For various reasons, instances of social injustice are in many cases more insidious than those of environmental injustice, because their effects are felt throughout American society. This is illustrated in Figure 7-1, which shows the percentages of various populations that live below the poverty level.[14] The percentages for black and Hispanic Americans are more than twice those for white Americans, which has unsustainable repercussions in many other public policy areas of society such as education and health care.

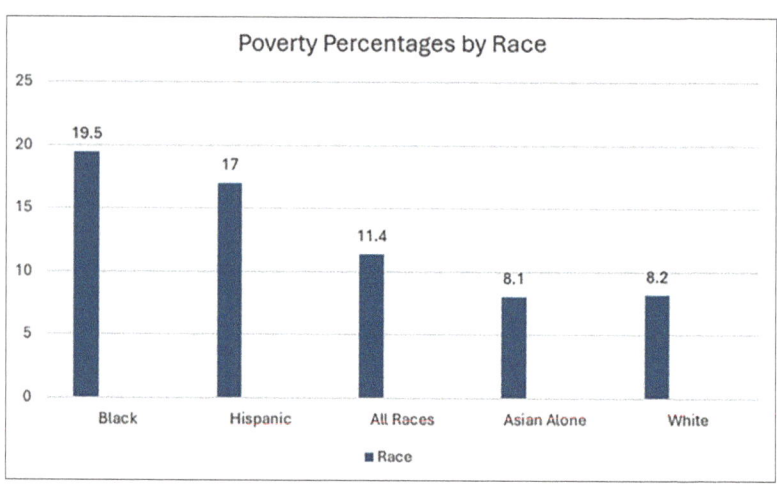

Figure 7-1
Percentage of population below the poverty level for various ethnic groups.
Source: Income, and Food Insecurity Data Reveal Continuing Racial Disparities. Center for American Progress

While instances of environmental injustice in the United States have decreased somewhat, largely due to federal and state regulation, those of social injustice appear to have risen. This is a result of its occurrence among people with racial, religious, economic, and other personal identifying characteristics. For example, as already mentioned, poorer families often must live in undesirable, often toxic, areas, and it is a well-known fact that women make only 79 cents for every dollar earned by men.[15] And it is also well-known that African American, Indigenous, and other People of Color make up a disproportionate amount of the homeless population compared to white people.[16]

III. Sustainable Development Impact

A. Definition of Sustainable Development

According to the Brundtland Report in 1987, there are three major concerns to be addressed in sustainable development: 1) the Environment; 2) the Economy; and 3) Social Equity. Neglecting any of these threatens—or even makes impossible—desirable sustainable development. And while the first two—the Environment and the Economy—often get the most attention, the third—Social Equity—is in some respects more important, as it encompasses so many aspects of life today throughout the world—racism, homelessness, hunger, wealth inequality, forced migration, and conflict. For this reason, social and environmental justice play a disproportionate role in advancing or hindering—sustainable development.

B. The United Nations Sustainable Development Goals

The United Nations 2030 Agenda for Sustainable Development includes 17 goals, and the first five: No Poverty, Zero Hunger, Good Health and Well-Being, Quality Education, and Gender Equality deal directly with social justice.

Probably most illustrative of social injustice is the issue of No Poverty. At a time when the concentration of wealth skews more and more to the wealthiest throughout the world and in the United States, there is no other issue of social justice which is as glaring as this. Oftentimes, when by accident of birth or circumstance one segment of society is favored to receive the benefits of that society in government, social position, or material comforts greater than would otherwise be indicated by merit, the well-being of that entire society is diminished. Even in those cases in which the wealth is earned by hard work and risk-taking, those less fortunate are deserving of no less respect simply because they are human beings. In any case, the sustainable development of that society is less than it would be otherwise, as shown by historical events such as the French Revolution.

Another physical demonstration of social injustice is the extent of hunger throughout the world, focused by the second Sustainable Development Goal—Zero Hunger. Simply because a child was born in Kenya or South Sudan is no reason why he or she should bear the physical trauma, and even illness and eventual death from not having enough to eat. And the incidence of hunger and poor nutrition is not limited to Third World nations. In the United States food deserts exist in many lower-income areas where people have little or no access to nutritious foods.

Similarly, because basic health care is readily available in the United States for those who can afford it or have it provided by their employers, it is more the exception than the rule in many Third World countries. Diseases and illness such as malaria, which have long been eradicated or controlled in developed countries, continue to plague those not so fortunate throughout the world. This Sustainable Development Goal—Global Health and Well-Being—seeks to address this social injustice by bringing the rudiments of health care to Third World countries through organizations such as the World Health Organization (WHO). Seldom has this injustice been make clearer than during the COVID-19 pandemic of 2020–2021 during which poorer countries had no access to otherwise readily available vaccines.

The fourth Sustainable Development Goal—Quality Education—is one which should mitigate social and environmental injustices. As more and more otherwise unfairly treated people receive the benefits of education, they are able to achieve the material and social benefits resulting from that education. The education of girls and young women in the Middle East time and again demonstrate lasting improvement in sustainable development, such as healthier families, more employment opportunities, and responsible use of resources.

And this, in turn, leads to improvement in the fifth UN Sustainable Development Goal—Gender Equality. Slowly, but surely, gone are the taboos of women working outside the home, which, in turn, leads to increased financial security for the family. Outward signs of the progress in gender equality include an increase in the number of women in government and the military, many becoming heads of state such as those in Finland, Sweden and New Zealand. And in 2022 a woman became the first to command an aircraft carrier in the U.S. Navy. All these point to advances in social justice and sustainable development.

Probably the most pertinent of the UN's Sustainable Development Goals with respect to social and environmental justice is the 16th— Peace, Justice, and Strong Institutions. For its focus is "on promoting peaceful and inclusive societies; providing access to justice for all; and building effective, accountable, and inclusive institutions at all levels," and is most pertinent for several reasons. One, this goal points to the failure in many parts of the world, such as the three nations of Central America (El Salvador, Honduras, and Guatemala) which have the most glaring examples of social injustice. Two, these injustices are so great that the populations of these countries are driven constantly to make their way north under the most life-threatening conditions to find a better life in the United States. And three, the goal points to possible solutions which should be taken by developed countries, especially the United States.[17]

IV. Leadership Opportunities in Addressing Social and Environmental Justice

A. Government

Possibly the best way to address social and environmental justice through government is the state and federal regulatory system.[18] And the best way to do this might be to consider, first, the ways in which regulation has failed to advance social and environmental justice.

The first of these is through the ineffective and obsolete laws passed by Congress. One need only to consider the polarization among Democrats and Republicans in the first decades of the 21st century. How else does one explain the failure to pass a voting rights act during this time frame except due to the political differences between the parties on this issue, the result being the disenfranchisement of many people of color in the United States? Or Congress' failure to pass the Build Back Better legislation in 2021-2022 which would have kept millions of children from lower socio-economic families from poverty?

Another failure of the regulatory system stems from restrictions on state and federal regulatory agencies that prevent them from implementing their responsibilities. This often results from the lack of funding necessary to carry out their mission, the explanation for which is given as budgetary, but too often this budget is balanced against the achievement of social justice for those without a voice.

Possibly the greatest hindrance to the achievement of social justice by regulatory action is the inordinate influence of corporations on government, including regulatory agencies. Nowhere is this as obvious as in the Supreme Court decision in *Citizens United* in 2010. While corporations had always exerted undue influence on government before that decision, it solidified the ability of corporations to influence government action – or inaction – in passing legislation favorable to corporations. and such legislation is more often beneficial to the rich and powerful than the marginalized citizens in society.

Finally, it is difficult for the marginalized members of society to participate in regulatory action. While no longer experienced outwardly in cities throughout the United States, the practice of Red Lining, which prevented African Americans from living in certain areas in many cities, has much to do with why lower socioeconomic groups are concentrated in certain areas to this day. Similarly, the complaints of people in Flint, Michigan, the population of which was predominantly African American or of lower socioeconomic status, were neglected until the harmful effects of its water supply were too deadly to ignore.

These observations then beg the question: What can be done to the U.S. regulatory system to make it more effective in advancing social and environmental justice? Perhaps a good start can be made by considering recommendations in each of the major systems of government: Congress, the regulatory agencies themselves, the courts, and state governments.

At the top of the list for Congress would have to be campaign finance reform. By removing the ability to influence legislation with campaign contributions by corporations and their lobbyists, the likelihood of such legislation benefitting all citizens rather than just the rich and powerful would be much greater. One very basic change in this regard would be to have all elections publicly financed. Currently, publicly financed elections in the U.S. is an option for candidates with some restrictions. Those who agree to certain spending limits will receive some amount taken from a fund financed by voters who agree to contribute three dollars in their tax return. Unfortunately, most candidates do not participate in public funding and choose to rely on the large donations of a few donors, or smaller donations from many donors (which is actually a more socially responsible alternative).

Something else Congress can do, which is related to campaign finance reform, would be a major revision to the budget process. Currently, the process is unduly cumbersome and usually reflects the support given by large donors and political control in the House and Senate. Again, it comes down to undue influence exercised by large corporations with available funding. The system of funding elections should be revised to eliminate the influence of corporate money.

Another way in which Congress can act to further social justice is by removing legislative gimmicks which tend to favor the rich and powerful. One of these is that provided by the Congressional Review Act (CRA). While on its face the act is impartial, it has too often been used to delay or eliminate the achievement of social justice, as it enables members of Congress to impose their own interpretation onto existing legislation.

With regard to regulatory agencies themselves, there are certain steps Congress and the president can take to ensure actions by them (the agencies) do not hinder social or environmental justice. In many cases the agencies must satisfy procedural obstacles such as cost/benefit analyses, which corporations can perform to their advantage, but these place an undue burden on the agencies. This burden consumes agency resources, and prevents them from acting in the interest of socially or economically marginalized citizens.

The federal government should account for the particular background and culture of lower socioeconomic and otherwise marginalized groups when establishing policies that affect everyone. Too often programs and laws are instituted which consider predominantly – or only – the perspectives of the rich and powerful. For example, the draft during the Vietnam War made it easier for well positioned or educated people to avoid service while people of color or those without a college education had to serve.

There should also be means to solicit and honor the perspectives of ordinary American citizens, especially people of color and those of lower socioeconomic position, when establishing facilities or infrastructure throughout the country. It is often easier to locate a toxic waste facility next to a community populated by people of color or lower socioeconomic means simply because they haven't been informed.

B. Businesses and Organizations

For-profit businesses often find it in their interest to speak up for social justice. For example, in the spring of 2022 the state legislature in Florida passed legislation which restricted the amount of information on homosexuality teachers could provide in public schools (the "don't say gay" law). The Disney Corporation, with its large amusement park in Orlando, publicly opposed the law, given the significant percentage of its own employees who identified as LGBTQ as well as a larger percentage of its customers. A similar stand was taken by other corporations throughout the United States, again probably motivated by the impact on business, but possibly also by sincere social equity reasons.

By far, though, the most common type of organization with impacts on social and environmental justice is the nonprofit. For every significant social or environmental issue, such as hunger, homelessness, climate change, or toxic waste, there is some nonprofit organization or Non-Governmental Organization (NGO) which is working to advance justice in that particular area.

C. Individual

Especially among the nonprofit organizations and NGOs, there are numerous individuals who, by their everyday actions in relating to others, advance social and environmental justice. For example, they can speak up at community events when it appears certain individuals or groups of people are being treated unfairly because of their racial or economic status. Or they can write letters to the editor of newspapers in which it appears these people are not given the same rights as others.

Individuals in public life, such as entertainers, those in government, or athletes, have a special role to play. Warranted or not, they hold positions of respect among the public, and their espousal of social or environmental issues can be particularly influential.

V. Examples of Leadership in Addressing Social and Environmental Justice

A. Government—The New Deal

Arguably, the best example of government's action in addressing social justice is President Franklin D. Roosevelt's leadership in advancing his suite of social programs included in The New Deal. Over the first 100 days of his first administration, he emphasized social programs which were focused on the "forgotten man," recognizing that the years leading up to his presidency were characterized by the wanton greed of corporations and the wealthy. This had led to massive unemployment and the collapse of the American economy. This recognition led to the creation of the Works Progress Administration (WPA) and the Civilian Conservation Corps (CCC), both of which were dedicated to getting America back to work after the damage caused by the Great Depression.

Under the WPA, 8.5 million jobs were created and numerous projects were undertaken by both the WPA and CCC to provide employment for Americans. Among these were 650,000 miles of new roads, 125,000 new buildings, 75,000 bridges, and 8,000 new parks. And to improve the stricken economy and address social justice, the National Recovery Administration (NRA) addressed codes, regulations, and revised business practices in banking and industry. These changes not only aided in getting the economy back on its feet, but led to improvements in child labor laws, collective bargaining, labor wages and working hours, and other changes which were designed to improve treatment of the American worker. All these issues required the leadership of Franklin D. Roosevelt to address some of the most pressing social justice challenges of his time, and the impact of these manifold programs, such as in Social Security, is felt to this day.

B. Business and Nonprofits—Ben & Jerry's Ice Cream

Mention social justice in business and the company which comes to mind for many people is Ben & Jerry's Ice Cream. Founded in a renovated gas station in Vermont in 1978, Ben & Jerry's Ice Cream has become synonymous with activism in social issues, especially social and environmental justice. Even after being acquired by Unilever in 2000, the founders insisted as part of the agreement the creation of an independent Board of Directors which would control branding and continue the company's social activism. Part of this agreement was the creation of the position Manager of Corporate Activism who would ensure the social justice emphasis of the company's founders would continue.

The social justice aspirations espoused by the company are best boldly proclaimed on its website under Movements We Support. Among them are voting rights, racial justice, LGBTQ rights, climate justice, and campaign finance reform. Especially in the area of racial justice, Ben & Jerry's has been especially active, as evidenced by its "We Must Dismantle White Supremacy" effort after the killing of George Floyd in 2020.

Lending credence to their work in these areas is their continuing recognition as a Fair Trade Company and Certified B Corporation. Both of these rating organizations require strict adherence to the principles of social and environmental justice, and their recognition is testimony to the leadership shown by Ben & Jerry's as a business organization.

C. Personal—Colin Kaepernick

Colin Kaepernick should be recognized for his efforts in promoting social justice and for what he has given up. Taking the San Francisco 49ers to the Super Bowl in 2013, he was an accomplished NFL quarterback with the promise of many more years as an active player. But he singlehandedly started a movement not only in the NFL but in society as well wherein athletes and other celebrities "took a knee" or otherwise protested the racism African Americans face in America today, and he paid a price. Even though he was a gifted athlete who displayed another type of leadership on the football field, it was the leadership he displayed in bringing to light racism in the NFL for which he will be best known.

References

1. *Social Justice in an Open World the Role of the United Nations*, 2006.
2. *WHAT IS SOCIAL JUSTICE?* The San Diego Foundation, 24 March 2016.
3. *The Five Principles of Social Justice*, Kent State University, July 30, 2020.
4. *7 Biggest Social Issues That Could Lead to Social Injustice*, Human Relations, Aug. 31, 2021.
5. Edward R. Berchick, Jessica C. Barnett, and Rachel D. Upton, *Health Insurance Coverage in the United States: 2018*, November 8, 2019.
6. *Learn About Environmental Justice*, United Stated Environmental Protection Agency (EPA).
7. Dana Alston, *The Summit: Transforming a Movement*, Race, Poverty & the Environment, Spring 2010.

8. Renee Skelton & Vernice Miller, *The Environmental Justice Movement*, March 17, 2016, National Renewal Defense Council.
9. Magali Flores Nunez, *Environmental Racism and Latino Farmworker Health in the San Joaquin Valley, California*, Harvard Journal of Hispanic Policy 2019.
10. Hailey Hansel, *How Social Justice and Environmental Justice are Intrinsically Connected*, January 11, 2018, Pachamama Alliance.
11. Melissa Denchak, *Flint Water Crisis: Everything You Need to Know*, March 8, 2018, NRDC.
12. Stephen B William, MD, MS, Yong Shan, PhD, Usama Jazzar, MD, et al, *Proximity of Oil Refineries and Risk of Cancer: A Population-Based Analysis*, National Library of Medicine, Oct 7, 2020.
13. Julie Snorek, *Tracking the battles for environmental justice: here are the world's top 10.*, The Conversation, June 4, 2018.
14. Statista Research Department, Statista, Sept 21, 2021.
15. Jessica Schieder and Elise Gould, *"Women's work" and the gender pay gap*, Economic Policy Institute, July 20, 2016.
16. Njeri Parker, *The Link Between Racism and Homelessness*, JOIN, July 23, 2020.
17. Kristin Cordell and Christine Li, *It's Time for the United States to Reengage with the SDGs, Starting with SDG 16*, Center for Strategic and International Studies (CSIS). April, 2021.
18. James Goodwin, *Regulation as Social Justice: A Crowdsourced Blueprint for Building a Progressive Regulatory System*, Center for Progressive Reform, September, 2019.

8

Immigration, Refugees, and Asylum Seekers

I. Definitions and Background

A. Immigration, Refugees, and Asylum Seekers[1]

Immigration occurs when a person living in one country moves to another country with the intention of living there permanently. The person is generally not a citizen of the country to which he or she emigrates, but they intend to become one eventually. The reasons for which this person emigrates are many, but usually it is a result of a desire to escape poverty, marrying someone in the country to which he is moving, an employment opportunity, or simply to fulfill a dream.

Refugees, on the other hand, leave their country due to severe violence or other conditions over which they have no control. Among these is famine or drought brought on by climate change, which have gotten worse in recent years in the Middle East and Africa as climate change has increased.

Asylum seekers desire refuge in another country from conditions of violence, perhaps not as severe as would make them refugees but still enough to make life in their country unbearable. Other reasons exist for migration such as government corruption and poverty in Central America, which led many to make the 1,000-mile journey on foot through Mexico to seek asylum in the United States.

While immigration is a simple aspect of demographics, there are ways in which it can affect sustainable development. The very existence of refugees reflects the worst behavior of humanity, such as war or the persecution of certain segments of population, or the worst effects of climate change which drive populations to do whatever they can to avoid famine, sickness, or personal danger. Closely related to the plight of refugees, are the conditions which drive many to seek asylum in other countries. While not officially recognized as refugees by the United Nations these conditions are so dire that asylum seekers go to great lengths to escape their countries. The need for sustainable leadership to address the causes of emigration is evident.

It is important to distinguish immigration policy from legislation meant to address treatment of refugees and those seeking asylum. In general, immigration policy specifies the numbers of immigrants that can be admitted to the United States, the provision of visas, rules concerning "green cards," and other administrative details. Refugees and those seeking asylum are regarded as special cases.

II. Extent Internationally and in the U.S.

A. Extent of Immigration Worldwide[2]

There were 280.6 million global migrants in 2020, which amounts to close to 4 percent of the worlds' population. This represents an increase from 3.2 percent in 2010, and 2.6 percent in 1960 as shown in Figure 8-1.

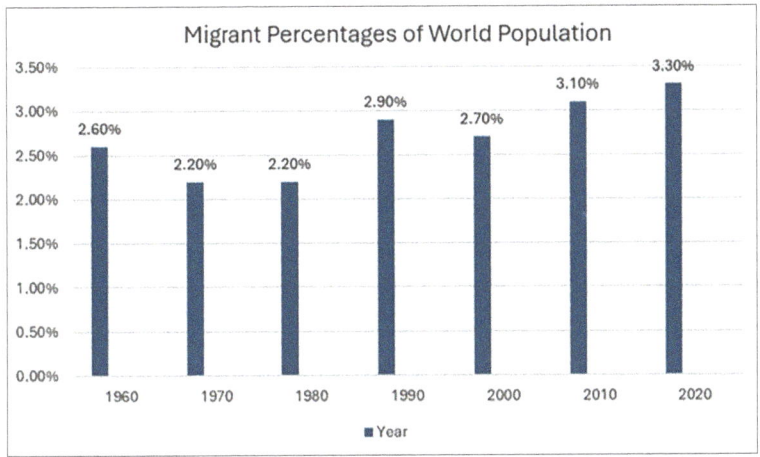

Figure 8-1 Numbers of international immigrants and percentage increases. Source: Pew Research Center Key facts about recent trends in global migration

As might be expected, the majority of these were in North America, accounting for 52 percent of the total, while the next largest percentage—18 percent—were those in North Africa and West Asia. In North America the United States accounted for 18 percent of the total, or 50.6 million in 2020, while Germany, Saudi Arabia, Russia, and the United Kingdom accounted for another 50.2 million.

B. Extent of Refugees

As of mid-2022 there were 27.1 million refugees worldwide. Almost 71 percent of these are from the following countries.

Syrian Arab Republic	6.8 million
Venezuela	5.6 million
Ukraine	5.4 million
Afghanistan	2.8 million
South Sudan	2.4 million

For various reasons – continued war in Syria and the war in Ukraine, to name just a couple – there's been a significant rise in in refugees the past five or ten years, as shown in the graph of Figure 8-2.

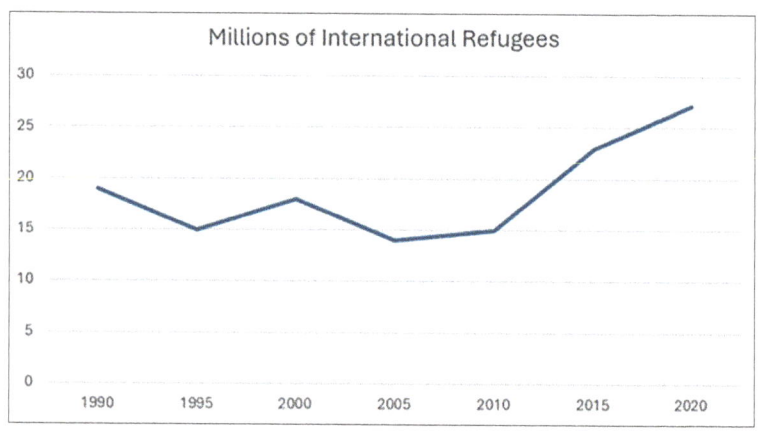

Figure 8-2 millions of refugees Source: UNHCR Global trends 2021.

By far, the largest number of refugees from any country comes from the Syrian Arabic Republic, or Syria.[3] In a population of over 16 million, 12 million are food insecure, which is an increase of 51 percent since 2019, for various reasons. In Syria the civil war that began in 2011 continues to the present day. Other contributing factors to the refugee crisis is violence related to the civil war and the collapse of infrastructure, also caused largely by social foment and the civil war. Especially affecting sustainable development of the country, is the civil war's impact on children, of which 2.4 million are unable to attend school. To make matters worse, in 2023 a 7.8 earthquake in Turkey, which claimed over 50,000 lives, occurred on the Turkish – Syrian border, which only added to the dire living conditions of refugees in Syria.

The nation with the next largest number of refugees is Venezuela at 5.6 million. Whereas violence, climate change, and war drove migration in other countries, the refugee crisis in Venezuela was caused more by the total economic collapse of the country than any other reason. In the years prior to 2015, when oil prices were high, the economy was relatively healthy and able to provide some semblance of a living standard to the Venezuelan people, but with the collapse of the market price of oil, the nation's Gross Domestic Product declined by 80 percent, which compares with the 28 percent reduction in the U.S. GDP in the Great Depression, and Germany's 50 percent decline in World War II.[4] Venezuela's socialist government responded by taking more control over the lives of its people, which prompted them (the people) to elect a National Assembly more amenable to the needs of the population. The government responded by imposing further restrictions on its people, which led to massive migration, mostly to the countries of Central America, but increasingly so to the United States, leading to the massive increase in refugees and those seeking asylum that we see today.

Closely following in the number of refugees worldwide is the number from Ukraine at 5.4 million, driven, of course, by the Russian invasion. But these numbers pale in comparison with the number of people displaced within their own countries as shown in Figure 8-3.

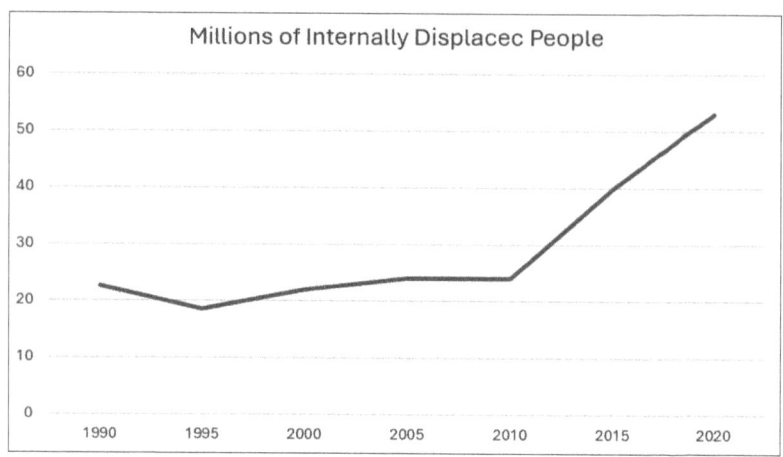

Figure 8-3 Millions of internally displaces people. Source UNHCR

One of the reasons for the significant increase in the past several years is most probably, again, the Russian invasion of Ukraine, which drove so many of its people to leave their homes.

C. Extent of Asylum Seekers

The number of asylum seekers is less than the number of refugees and internally displaced persons, totaling 4.9 million in 2022, but it has gotten considerable attention, especially in the last two decades of the twenty-first century. This is due largely to the boat crossings in the Mediterranean from Africa to Europe and in the Caribbean from Cuba to the U.S. A tragic example of this was the sinking of a boat in the Mediterranean off the coast of Italy carrying upwards of 200 asylum seekers from Afghanistan and Pakistan on February 26, 2023.[5] More than 62 people died, including 12 children, but it is feared more than 100 have perished. Since 2014 more than 26,000 asylum seekers have died trying to make the trip across the Mediterranean from Africa or the Middle East.

The flow of asylum seekers at the southern border of the United States has gotten significant attention due to its political impact and the failure of Congress to enact an effective immigration policy. This flow is worthy of special consideration as its reasons are illustrative of the increasing flow of asylum seekers throughout the world.

This (the flow of asylum seekers) has been driven predominantly by those fleeing the Central American countries of Guatemala, Honduras, and El Salvador located south of Mexico and north of Nicaragua. The distance from these countries through Mexico to the U.S. border is about 1,000 miles and for various reasons thousands of asylum seekers facilitated by human traffickers endure harsh conditions to make the journey. Among these are socioeconomic conditions, natural disasters, security conditions, and governance.[6]

With regard to socioeconomic conditions, economic power and land ownership in these countries have existed primarily among a select, privileged group of people, leading to stark economic inequality in the population. What's more, between 35 and 44 percent of the population in these countries is under the age of twenty, which means there are more and more people seeking the limited employment opportunities that are available. As a result, families seeking jobs are willing to travel the 1,000 miles plus to look for work in the U.S.

Other factors driving individuals and families to leave Central America were environmental, especially those related to climate change. The region has been especially hot and dry during the last twenty years, causing extended droughts which has made farming difficult. Those depending on the coffee industry have been especially hard hit.

In addition, COVID-19 and hurricanes Eta and Iota in 2020 have taken their toll on the economy. Along with the severe economic contraction, the number of food insecure people in Central America increased from 2.2 million in 2019 to 6.4 million in 2021 driving thousands to leave their countries to head north.

Not the least of the factors driving those to seek asylum is violence and the lack of security in the region. One of the main drivers for this insecurity is the fact that the region is on the main route for drug trafficking from South America to the United States. Rival traffickers compete for the ability to ship drugs to the U.S., and the citizens of Guatemala, Honduras, and El Salvador are caught in the middle and fall victim to the violence that comes with the drug trade. Related to this is the violence among local gangs such as Mara Salvatrucha (MS-13) and the 18th street gang (M-18) which are constantly competing in local conflicts.

Finally, a major reason for so much of the population wanting to leave these countries and seek asylum in the United States is governance in their countries—or lack thereof. Autocratic rule is more typical in these countries than democratic rule, and as a result, government is slow to correct socioeconomic inequality and damage from natural disasters. This is compounded by inadequate revenues from taxes, as exemplified by the low gross domestic product (12.4 percent) in Guatemala—the lowest in Latin America. Also, corruption is rampant, preventing these governments from devoting needed resources to the public sector to correct the many societal problems which are driving populations to seek asylum in other countries.

These are among the reasons why the flow of migrants at the U.S. border are at record highs, as shown by Figure 8-4.

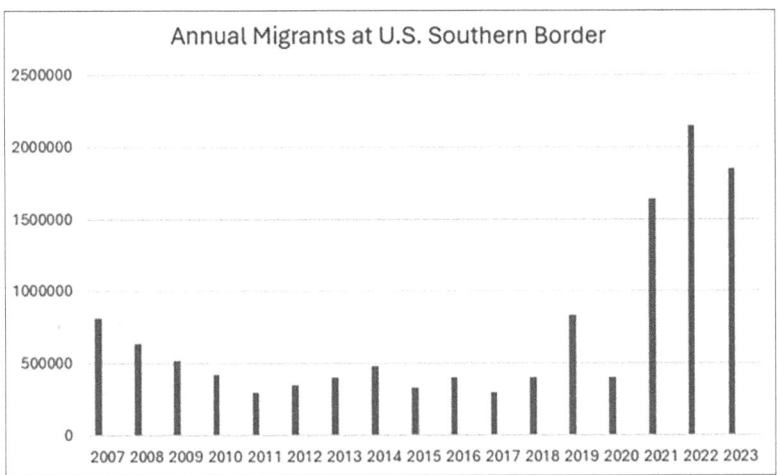

Figure 8-4 Annual migrant encounters at U.S. southern border. Source: U.S. Customs and Border Protection.

III. Sustainable Development Impact

A. Environment[7]

The most obvious impact of refugees and asylum seekers on sustainable development is its effect on the environment. Among these effects is that of deforestation driven by refugees' attempts to eke out a living in their dire circumstances. For example, during the refugee crisis in Tanzania in the period of 1994–1996, 167 square kilometers of forest was so affected, as refugees sought to provide a living for themselves. In 1994 when refugees returned to Zimbabwe, 58 percent of the land surrounding their encampment was deforested. Similar detrimental effects on water and natural resources have occurred as a result of refugees attempting to just live. Also, there is increased pollution from refugee communities due to inhabitants burning whatever is available, including trash and forest growth, for heating and cooking purposes.

B. UN Sustainability Goals[8]

A more explicit statement of the impacts of refugees and asylum seekers on sustainable development is the way they affect the seventeen sustainable development goals the United Nations published in 2015.

The first of these goals is the elimination of poverty, and toward this end the UN has developed the Poverty Alleviation Coalition. This Coalition intentionally seeks participants with specific skills in poverty reduction and those with experience in developing countries and skills in working with refugees. The Coalition uses a proven model for poverty reduction known as The Graduation Approach and the Bangladesh Rural Advancement Committee has achieved a 75 percent reduction in poverty since its founding in 2002.[9]

Another challenge to refugees and those seeking asylum is that presented by the physical conditions in which they live. Forced to live in squalid camps of limited space without the basic necessities of life, those living under such conditions often contract physical and mental illnesses as well.[10] One way to address such debilitating conditions is the UN Refugee Agency's Mental Health and Psychosocial Support (MHPSS) unit. Not only do physical ailments affect the health of those living in these camps, but forced living under these conditions, which are nevertheless often an improvement on their previous lives, takes a serious toll on their mental health. And MHPSS provides counseling and mental health services which improve the lives of refugees and those seeking asylum.

The fourth UN sustainable development goal is Quality Education. Forty-eight percent of all refugees who are of school age do not attend school, and only three percent of all the world's refugees are able to receive a higher education. Without a sound education, children in developing countries, especially those living as refugees, will be unable to contribute to sustainable development as they grow older.

This is especially true in those countries in which only half the population are able to contribute to this development, as is the case in those countries where girls and women do not receive the same opportunity as boys and men. For this reason, the UN has made gender equality a priority, and one of its sustainable development goals. Only when all genders can participate equally in all the benefits, opportunities, and responsibilities afforded to all will their nations achieve this development.

It almost goes without saying that one of the most necessary and basic needs of any nation and its people is clean water and sanitation. Yet one of the most glaring tragedies in refugee camps is the lack of this basic need. Addressing this, the UN has pledged at least twenty liters of potable water for each person in refugee camps. One very simple, but effective, approach has been the construction of "tippy taps" in refugee camps with little or no access to potable water. These admittedly crude devices consist of plastic containers containing a hole which may be opened and closed with an inserted stick to permit the flow of water without anyone's hands touching the container. This allows access to water for hand washing or other hygiene purposes without spreading disease by touch. UN leadership has installed over 300 such tippy taps and more than 200 refugees have been trained to build them.

Another sustainable life necessity that is often not available to refugees and those seeking asylum is affordable and clean energy, sustainable development goal number seven. Over 90 percent of those living in refugee camps have little or no electricity, and in order to cook their food, women must travel to gather firewood for energy. Aside from being physically demanding, such trips often present danger to the women making them. In Somalia one solution has been to make briquettes from an otherwise invasive tree to provide a ready source of energy and forego the laborious process of finding firewood. Not only does this satisfy the need for energy, but the process of making the briquettes also provides a source of income for those making them.

The eighth UN sustainable development goal is providing Decent Work and Economic Growth. For such development to occur, not only do refugees and those seeking asylum have to satisfy the needs of the present, but they must have some assurance that they will be able to satisfy the needs of their families in the future. Because they do have these basic physical needs there is a demand for assistance, and companies working with the UN are able to provide training and resources to accomplish this.

This requires a structured approach to identify opportunities and provide the resources and training for decent work and economic growth. Toward this end the UN has adopted the ninth sustainable development goal – Industry, Innovation, and Infrastructure. One example of this is the Innovation Lab in Jordan, which assists refugees in developing technologies conducive to sustainable development. Recently the lab developed a robotic sanitation dispenser from Lego bricks which not only provides a hands-free sanitizer but possibly a product which can assist the refugees' economic development.

While inequality is pervasive in so many segments of society such as housing, health care, and employment, it is especially harmful to LGBTQ persons in refugee communities. This is because not only do refugees and asylum seekers lack the basic requirements for a healthy life and are treated with disdain in society, but LGBTQ persons face even greater prejudices in refugee communities. Recognizing this, the UN Refugee Agency has formed a network which specifically seeks to address these prejudices against LGBTQ persons. One example is the transgender woman who had to leave Venezuela and flee to Chile where she had the support of this network. There she received assistance in her transition and employment and was able to continue her education.

In a very real sense refugees and asylum seekers provide the UN opportunities to implement its eleventh sustainable development goal – Sustainable Cities and Communities. Since the majority of the world's 26 million refugees settle in urban areas, they are able, just by living their lives sustainably, to shape these urban areas into sustainable cities. The UN Refugee Agency is making this happen through its Cities of Light program by supporting the efforts of refugees to live sustainably in major cities throughout the world. For example, the Benang (Indonesian for "thread") Project in Jakarta provides training for refugees in designing, making patterns, and tailoring clothing to help them become productive and contributing residents of the city. Integrating refugees into the economy of Jakarta helps to make it one of the Cities of Light. Similarly, the City of Altena, Germany, suffered from a dwindling population in recent years, but welcomed 450 asylum seekers who brought new skills to its once thriving manufacturing industry and contributed to the city's sustainable development.

While many developed countries consume a disproportionate share of the earth's natural resources, asylum seekers and refugees counter this with an emphasis on Responsible Consumption and Production. The UN Refugee Agency has worked with Sudan's Forests National Corporation (FNC) to counter deforestation and promote the growth of new saplings, protecting the environment and promoting responsible use of these natural resources, contributing to sustainable development of this country.

The UN.s thirteenth Sustainable Goal – Climate Action – is especially pertinent to asylum seekers since climate change is often the immediate cause of those seeking asylum or those becoming refugees.[11] Consider the drought and resulting famine in 2021–2022 in which a million people have been displaced due to the inability to raise crops from lack of rain caused by climate change.[12] Nine hundred children under the age of five are among the thousands who have died from malnutrition during the famine in Somalia, with no climate relief in sight at the time.

There is also the issue of flooding caused by climate change in low lying Bangladesh.[13] More than 130 rivers meander across the country, changing course erratically brought on by erosion and sea level rise due to climate change. The flight of asylum seekers is so great that more than 2,000 enter Dhaka, the capital city, from flooded villages every day. By 2050 it is estimated that Bangladesh will have one third of all the internally displaced asylum seekers in South Asia.

The fourteenth UN Sustainable Development Goal is—Life Below Water—which addresses pollution in the world's waterways and how refugees are helping to clean them.[14] There are now 247,499 refugees and asylum seekers in Egypt and recently 50 from Syria, Sudan, Ethiopia, Somalia and Yemen joined 800 local volunteers to clean up a segment of the Nile River which provides 90 percent of the fresh water to the Egyptian people. Activities such as this not only contribute to satisfying the fresh water needs of the host country but promote better relationships between the local population and refugees, both of which contribute to sustainable development.

Refugees and asylum seekers also play an important role in the fifteenth UN Sustainable Development Goal—Life on Land—or concern for, and preservation of, the natural environment.

Sustainable development is significant to refugees and asylum seekers both for their safety and health and for protection of the environment itself. One Bangladesh settlement lies on a wild elephant migratory route between Myanmar and Bangladesh, and refugees are frequently attacked by migrating elephants and their homes destroyed. To protect both the refugees and migrating elephants, the UN Refugee Agency and International Union for Conservation of Nature established a "tusk force" to alert refugees of the passage of the elephants.[15] This action and others is a positive sustainable development step for both refugees and the environment.

The very essence of being a refugee or one seeking asylum is the reality of not having a home or nation to be part of, and the UN's sixteenth Sustainable Development Goal—Peace, Justice, and Strong Institutions—addresses this. Too often citizens from any country take for granted the benefits of being part of a nation, such as the ability to get a passport, employment opportunities, medical care, or any of countless advantages that depend on being part of that nation. Such benefits directly affect a nation's (and individual's) ability to achieve sustainable development, and the UN is in a position to work with member nations to grant citizenship to refugees and those seeking asylum.

The UN recognizes the interrelationship of these goals and the necessity of its members cooperating to achieve them in its seventeenth Sustainable Development Goal –Partnerships for the Goals. For example, there's an obvious connection between the seventh and the thirteenth goals—Affordable and Clean Energy and Climate Action—since achievements on the former will lead to success on the latter. Similar connections exist among the other goals, enhancing the likelihood of achieving sustainable development in issues affecting refugees and those seeking asylum.

IV. Leadership Opportunities in Addressing Immigration, Refugees, and Asylum Seekers

A. Government

One of the main ways governments can show leadership in immigration and the way refugees and asylum seekers are treated is through government policy and legislation. For years the U.S. Congress has tried to pass immigration reform without success. Unfortunately, even discussions of immigration, and specifically the flow of asylum seekers at the southwest border of the U.S., has become a hotly debated political issue. Consider advocates who shout, "Build the Wall!" Such statements are often driven by xenophobia and hate and are essentially counterproductive. Fortunately, there are many in government who work tirelessly to pass legislation to reform national policy on immigration.

Other leadership opportunities exist in the very countries from which citizens flee due to government corruption, persecution, and flagrant economic inequality. These opportunities include striving for economic opportunity, promoting public safety, and protecting human rights. Taking advantage of these opportunities will depend on those in key positions in government and their sincere desire to exercise leadership in sustainable development.

B. Corporations and Nonprofit Organizations

Critical to achieving success in assisting those seeking asylum and those living as refugees are those corporations with an international footprint. Especially in those countries in which large corporations are exploiting native populations in oil exploration or mining of precious minerals, these corporations and their shareholders have a moral responsibility to treat their workers fairly. A major reason for those seeking asylum in other countries is economic inequality often stemming from corporate employment practices.

Almost too numerous to mention are the many nonprofits and NGOs, which dedicate themselves to specific concerns of refugees, such as hunger, human trafficking, and medical care. At the top of this list is the UN Refugee Agency (UNHCR), which coordinates the efforts of other nonprofits in addressing the mistreatment of refugees throughout the world.

C. Individual

On any given day there are numerous individuals at the San Ysidro border crossing in San Diego seeking to provide transportation to asylum seekers to connect with friends or relatives in the United States, or just to show moral support for their efforts.

Another way individuals can show leadership in sustainable development is to support asylum seekers and refugees in public advocacy, if only by writing letters to local newspapers. Too often voices espousing hatred for immigrants are the loudest, and public support for the humane treatment of asylum seekers and refugees can help to neutralize this behavior.

Finally, for every segment of UNHCR, there are individuals who have taken it upon themselves to address a specific issue of maltreatment of refugees in Third World countries, such as hunger, human trafficking, or providing clean water.

V. Examples of Leadership in Addressing Social and Environmental Justice

A. Government

Notwithstanding the failure of government to address immigration, it has done some things to provide humane treatment of asylum seekers and refugees. One of these is DACA, or Deferred Action for Childhood Arrivals. Conceived and introduced under President Barack Obama in 2012, and implemented by Homeland Security Secretary Janet Napolitano, the program enabled certain undocumented individuals from other nations to remain and work in the United States without citizenship. To qualify under DACA, among other things, the immigrants were required: 1) to be thirty-one years of age by June 15, 2012; 2) to have arrived in the United States before their sixteenth birthday; 3) to have lived continuously in the United States from June 15, 2007; and several other requirements, most notably, to have not been convicted of a felony.

The impact of DACA on sustainable development is undeniable. Surveys have shown that as of 2020, 202,500 of the almost 600,000 DACA recipients were "essential critical infrastructure workers."[16] These include those working in health care such as nursing and psychiatric and personal care, and in education and food-industries, clearly positions which advance sustainable development.

Another way in which government leadership specifically addressed immigration was through the Immigration Reform and Control Act, supported and signed by Ronald Reagan in 1986. As initially proposed, the Act granted amnesty to illegal immigrants who were living in the United States before 1982 and imposed tighter restrictions on employers who hired workers here illegally.

While the latter provision (employers' restrictions) was taken from the bill before its passage, its amnesty provision for almost three million immigrants in the United States demonstrated the governmental leadership which would be necessary to address the issue of immigration in the United States.

B. Businesses and Nonprofit Organizations[17]

1. IKEA

Foremost among IKEA's efforts to assist refugees is to simply recognize they exist, and the contribution they (the refugees) can make to sustainable development. IKEA and other large companies, such as Apple, Microsoft, and Amazon, have a powerful voice and can influence public opinion toward refugees. This is especially true given the tendency of some governments to look the other way when it comes to the treatment of refugees.

IKEA has also recognized the importance of addressing both the short-term needs (food, clothing, shelter) and long-term needs (education, employment, business skills) of refugees. At the same time, IKEA is aware of the specific skills the refugees themselves bring to the company, such as native language and cultural familiarity. In this regard, IKEA has made inclusive hiring corporate policy, giving as much attention to hiring refugees as any other group, in recognition of the fact that they (refugees) often have their own specific skills.

Given its international presence, IKEA recognizes the importance of implementing its refugee policies globally. In that way it can address the treatment of refugees more sustainably in countries in which it would not otherwise occur. This, in turn, will advance sustainable development internationally rather than in just selected countries.

2. Adidas

Given its headquarters in Germany, it's appropriate that Adidas is progressive in its treatment of refugees, as that country has been at the forefront in doing so. Among the distinguishing characteristics of this treatment by Adidas in its policy on the integration of refugees into its company. So focused on this aspect is Adidas that it has established a *Wir Zusammen* ("Us Together") initiative which is a two-year course of integration, attended by students from different countries, which includes a four-week internship at Adidas. This internship assists participants in language training, intercultural development, and the preparation of employment applications and resumes. It is noteworthy that Adidas does not pay these interns, but it does pay into a fund which goes to providing language training and intercultural development.

To accelerate the integration of refugees into the German culture, Adidas provides three days of leave to its own employees who volunteer to work with refugees in this effort. This not only contributes to the integration of refugees, but encourages the acceptance of refugees by native Germans.

To ensure the success of these programs, Adidas monitors their effect over time. Toward this end, the company has created a position which specifically monitors this progress, and a previous refugee from Eretria from thirty years ago currently fills this position.

Both IKEA and Adidas are examples of what businesses can do in providing leadership in sustainable development for refugees and those seeking asylum.

C. Individual

In 1940 the Emergency Rescue Committee sent a young American journalist named Varian Fry to Marseilles where he set up a refugee rescue operation working out of a hotel. Only thirty-two at the time, Fry helped more than 1,500 refugees escape occupied France, and provided aid to 2,000 others. When the Nazis learned of this, they expelled Fry from the country in 1941.

For his achievements France awarded him the French Legion of Honor in 1967, and Israel gave him the "Righteous Among Nations" medal in 1996—the first American to be so honored.

References

1. Mark Blackwood, *Migration vs. Immigration: Understanding the Nuances*, August 20, 2020. The wordpoint.
2. Jeanne Batalova, *Top Statistics on Global Migration and Migrants*, July 21, 2022, Migration Policy Institute.
3. Kathryn Reid, *Syrian refugee crisis; Facts, Figures, and How to Help*, World Vision, July 12, 20223.
4. Stuart Anderson, *Venezuelans Propelled to U.S. by Crisis, Not Immigration Policy*, Forbes, December 14, 2022.
5. Davide Ghiglione & Alexandra Fouché, *Italy migrant boat shipwreck: More than 100 people feared dead*, BBC, February 27, 2023.
6. Peter J. Meyer, *Central American Migration: Root Causes and U.S. Policy*, Congressional Research Service. Dec. 12, 2022.
7. *Refugees and the Environment*, The UN Refugee Agency, January 1, 2001.
8. *Deanna Bitetti and Sarah Schafer, 17 overlooked ways refugees are leading on sustainable development*, UN Refugee Agency, Sep. 17, 2020.
9. *Poverty Alleviation Coalition*, UNHCR The UN Refugee Agency.
10. Rasheed Hussein Rasheed, *Refugees deliver mental health services* to locked down camps in Iraq, UNHCR The UN Refugee Agency, July 8, 2020.
11. Opira Bosco Okot, *'As a refugee, I have seen the impacts of the climate crisis up close'*, The UN Refugee Agency, 9 November 2022.
12. Omar Faruk, *Prolonged drought brings famine and fear to Somalia*, PBS News Hour, October 5, 2022.
13. AL-EMRUN GARJON and JULHAS ALAM, *Climate Migration: Flooding forces family to flee*, AP NEWS, August 17, 2022.

14. Yasmine El Demerdash, *Refugees in Egypt pitch in to fight plastic pollution along the Nile*, The UN Refugee Agency, July 11, 2019.
15. Caroline Gluck, *'Tusk force' set up to protect refugees and elephants in Bangladesh*, The UN Refugee Agency, March 2, 2018.
16. *Deferred Action for Childhood Arrivals (DACA): An Overview*, American Immigration Council.
17. Denise Delaney, *Business Leadership on Refugees: IKEA and Adidas, SustainAbility's Radar magazine*, March 18, 2017.

9

Health and Health Care

I. Definitions and Background

A. Health and Well-Being

The WHO in 1948 gave this definition of health: "health is a state of complete physical, mental, and social well-being and not merely the absence of disease or infirmity."[1] WHO expanded this definition in 1986 with the following: "A resource for everyday life, not the objective of living, Health is a positive concept emphasizing social and personal resources, as well as physical capacities," the intent being that good health is not just staying alive, but having good health is a resource for a full, productive, and enjoyable life. More specifically, physical health (setting aside for a moment the special case of mental health) exists when all bodily functions, organs, and their operation are performing at their optimum.

At its most basic level, good health is simply the absence of physical pain or illness. What can be more important than simply not hurting? Beyond that, the healthy individual experiences that sense of well-being that comes from not being distracted by issues endemic to the human body (or mind), such as colds, fever, exhaustion, and so on. In other words, good health is simply feeling good.

Perhaps even more important is the fact that good health enables one to engage in physical activities which themselves provide so many benefits.[2] Among these are immediate benefits such as the ability to think clearly and focus as often occurs just after exercise. One may find himself or herself more relaxed and able to sleep better after beginning a program of regular exercise.

Another benefit of regular physical activity is weight management. Since the body burns calories just by moving—actually even when standing still, or even sleeping—it stands to reason that any form of physical exercise will increase the calories burned, and result in weight loss, assuming a reasonable diet. And the ability to exercise is heavily dependent on one's health to begin with. What's more, the likelihood of maintaining the weight loss is much greater with a regular exercise routine. For long term weight management, the Centers for Disease Control and Prevention recommends 150 minutes per week of moderate physical activity.

A number of diseases and illnesses have been shown to occur less frequently with regular exercise. Foremost among these are cardiovascular diseases such as heart disease, strokes, and high blood pressure, as physical activity conditions the heart, veins, and arteries to operate for maximum performance. Even many cancers, including lung, colon, stomach, and breast cancer occur less often in those who exercise regularly. Not only does physical exercise improve one's chances of avoiding these types of cancer, but it improves the quality of life of those who survive cancer.

As one grows older, one notices aches and pains, especially from living a sedentary life in an office or behind a computer. To forego this, or at least delay the onset, it's important to strengthen one's joints, bones, and muscles. The best way to do this is through physical exercise. Along with a proper diet, exercise enables one to enjoy social activities such as cycling, hiking, and tennis, which themselves promote good physical health.

Another benefit of regular physical activity is improved balance which can help prevent falls resulting from simple activities such as climbing stairs or walking the dog. As one ages a person's sense of balance often deteriorates, but there are numerous types of physical exercises that can improve balance. If one does experience a fall, the likelihood of broken bones is reduced by engaging in physical exercise. And if one does break a bone or strains a muscle, the recovery period is shortened by having engaged in physical activity and exercise.

Studies have also shown that physical activity leads to a longer life. In fact, one study has shown that moderate to rigorous physical activity could prevent up to110,000 deaths a year in those forty years old and older.[3]

Finally, physical activity and exercise can lead to less painful chronic conditions such as arthritis and reduced heart disease in those with Type 2 diabetes. And those with disabilities are able to achieve a higher level of independence with regular physical activity and exercise.

With so many life issues dependent on the ability to exercise and engage in physical activity, it's important to consider those factors which do, in fact, lead to sound physical health.[4] Perhaps foremost among these are genetic factors. Those fortunate enough to have healthy parents can usually count on having sound physical health. But environmental factors also influence one's health. Among these are socioeconomic factors which influence one's living conditions, access to health care, and the financial position of one's family. Also, there are factors of the physical environment, such as the presence of infectious disease and harmful pollution. Finally, one's health can be affected by personal behavior, such as participation in dangerous sports or activities.

What can be done to increase the chances of having good health? Actually, there are many things one can do, such as participating in regular physical exercise, including cardiovascular and strength exercises. But it's also important to eat a balanced, nutritious diet, and to be screened regularly for diseases which may threaten one's health. And the value of having a purpose in life and maintaining a positive outlook cannot be overemphasized.

According to the WHO, mental health is a state of mental well-being that enables people to cope with the stresses of life, realize their abilities, learn well and work well, and contribute to their community. It is an integral component of health and well-being that underpins our individual and collective abilities to make decisions, build relationships, and shape the world we live in. Mental health is a basic human right. And it is crucial to personal, community, and socioeconomic development.

There are many reasons mental health is so important.[5] For one, it's critical in maintaining relationships with others. How often is relating to others hampered by hostility brought on by poor mental health or failure to understand and empathize with others simply due to a mental condition? Also, mental health is often a predictor of emotional well-being. It's difficult to maintain a positive outlook on life if there is some underlying reason such as anxiety, or even mild depression preventing an otherwise positive outlook. The result is a general feeling of dissatisfaction when one is affected by poor mental health. In the extreme, depression and poor mental health can even lead to suicide.

Even if poor mental health is not apparent to the one experiencing it, the effects are often felt by others who are victimized by the one with a mental health condition. How else can one explain the incidence of mass murders, rapes, or beatings except by the presence of so many in society experiencing sociopathic tendencies brought on by poor mental health?

On a more practical level, research shows that those experiencing some degree of poor mental health are less productive. In the extreme, research published in the American Journal of Psychiatry has shown that those experiencing a serious mental health condition earn forty percent less than those who do not. This, in turn, causes lost productivity which has a negative effect on the overall economy.

Aside from the higher incidence of crime due to the poor mental health of some, there is a general deterioration in society brought on by poor mental health. Children raised in families in which there is abuse by parents experiencing mental health deficiencies tend to normalize such behavior and continue it in raising their own families. This has a negative effect on society by spreading such interpersonal behavior.

On perhaps the most basic level, poor mental health prevents one from enjoying the quality of life experienced by those of sound mental health. Beset by anxiety, depression, unreasonable fear, or other indicators of poor mental health, a person is unable to appreciate the company of others or enjoy the simpler pleasures of life. Unfortunately, those experiencing deteriorated mental health are not able to realize they are missing the simple joys of life due to the state of their mental health. This calls for the assistance of therapists, counselors, or other mental health professionals to guide them in their search for better mental health.

B. Health Care

The WHO recognizes six characteristics of quality health care.[6] First it must *be safe and effective*. Not only must it not be harmful to the user, but it must work. In other words, it can reasonably be expected to cure illnesses and heal injuries. Secondly, it should be *people-centered*, or intended to address the needs and desires of the individual for whom the care is being provided throughout his or her life. Thirdly, the care must be *timely*, or be available when most need it, or as soon as possible. Fourth, it should be *equitable*, or available to anyone who needs it, regardless of their race, position in society, or their ability to pay. Fifth, quality health care should be *integrated*, or designed to address the health needs of a person throughout his or her life. And finally, it should be *efficient*, in that enough resources are used to provide quality health care but, insofar as reasonable, no more.

There are four major health care systems: 1) the Beveridge model; 2) the Bismarck model; 3 the National Health Insurance model; and 4) the Uninsured model.[7] These models differ primarily in the way they are funded and who actually provides the health care.

The Beveridge model was first proposed in Great Britain in 1942, and later actually implemented in 1946 with the Health Service Act. Under this model all health care is funded by taxation of the general population, and delivery is controlled by the British government with a few exceptions in which private entities control the delivery of health care. In addition to Great Britain, other countries following this model are Finland, New Zealand, and Spain.

The second type of health care follows the Bismarck model which was introduced in the German Empire, now Germany, by its first chancellor, Otto von Bismarck. Under this model, both the funding and delivery of health care are provided by private donations from required payroll deductions at companies which are termed "sickness funds." These funds are then used to reimburse companies which actually provide the health care. Countries which use this model include France, Japan, South Korea, and the Czech Republic.

The National Health Insurance Model has elements of both the Beveridge and Bismarck Models. Under it, government taxes individuals (like the Beveridge Model), but then uses these taxes to reimburse private organizations which actually provide the health care (similar to the Bismarck Model). An example of this is Canada.

Finally, as the name implies, under the Uninsured Model, it is up to individuals to provide their own health care. Obviously, those who can afford it—generally in more affluent countries—have the best health care that money can buy, but unfortunately, even in the United States, many go without health care. In Third World countries this is even more so, and the general health and well-being of the population reflects this.

II. Extent Worldwide and in the U.S.

A. Health and Well-Being

According to research funded by the National Institutes of Health in 2012, and documented in a report entitled *Shorter Lives, Poorer Health*, Americans fared worse than almost any industrialized nation in the world in life expectancy. The research looked at the population as a whole and considered life expectancy in five different areas including the public health system, individual behaviors such as diet and smoking, social factors such as income, the physical environment, including transportation, and public policies. In every one of these areas, Americans did worse in terms of life expectancy than every other industrialized nation, despite its advanced health care systems.

These results were surprising, to say the least, but the results were confirmed by a study in 2022 by the Centers for Disease Control and Prevention and the Organization for Economic Co-operation and Development (OECD). The results are shown in Figure 9-1, Clearly, since 1980 Americans have consistently had a lower life expectancy than citizens of other industrialized countries, and this difference has been increasing to where it is today. In 2021 those in other similarly advance nations could expect to live until 82.4 years of age, but Americans live more than six years fewer to the age of 76.1, and these differences are independent of race and socioeconomic class. About the only age group for which this difference in life expectancy is not so striking is for those above 75 years of age. For other age groups in general this difference in life expectancy is indeed thought provoking.

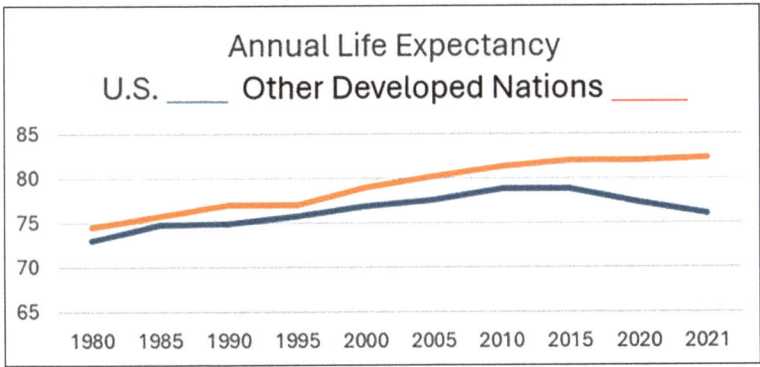

Figure 9-1. Expected life expectancy from 1980 to 2021 among industrialized nations.
Source: Petersen-KFF Health System Tracker, Credit Ashley/NPR.

There are many reasons for this difference, none of which predominates, although there are certainly many reasons indicative of the American life style. For one, according to the Organization for Economic Cooperation and Development (OECD), the incidence of obesity in young people in the United State is much greater in the United States than in other industrialized nations. With increased obesity the occurrence of diabetes and heart disease is much greater than in those who are not overweight. The difference among industrialized nations is striking, with the rate of obesity in the United States more than twice as high as that in Denmark, France, Norway, Japan, and Switzerland.

Another factor in the reduced life expectancy in the United States is the prevalence of gun violence probably due to the fact that there are more guns in this country than people. Especially concerning and directly contributing to reduced life expectancy are the deaths among children from guns. As shown in Figure 9-2, deaths among children and teens rose 50 percent from 2019 to 2021.[8] These deaths have a direct impact on life expectancy because, by definition, they occur predominantly among the younger population.

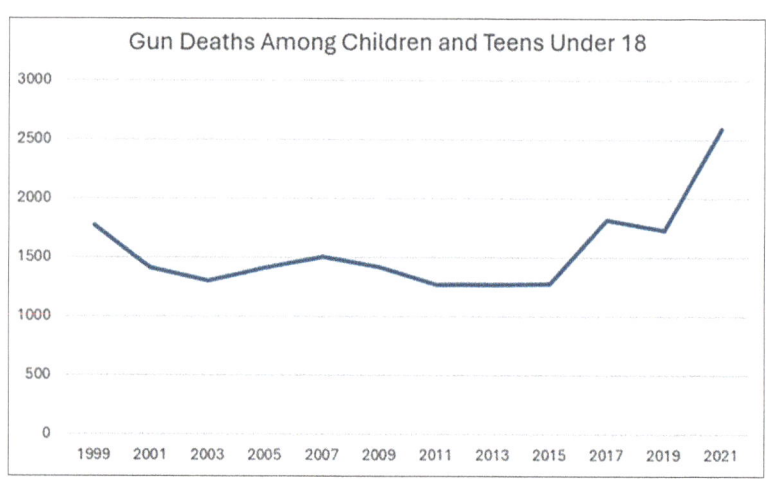

Figure 9-2 Gun deaths among children and teens under eighteen.
Source: Pew Research Center

If possible, even more striking is the contribution to reduced life expectancy than obesity and gun deaths is that by drug disorders.[9] As Figure 9-3 shows, on a drug-related death per million of population, the United States is far above other high-income countries at 322 with Scotland being the only country coming even close at 264. Except for Canada, at 209, Scotland at 264, and Northern Ireland at 112, all of the others are well under 100. There are many reasons for this difference in deaths by drug abuse, which this chapter will consider later, but suffice it to say, such abuse, especially among young people, almost assuredly is partly to blame for reduced life expectancy in the US.

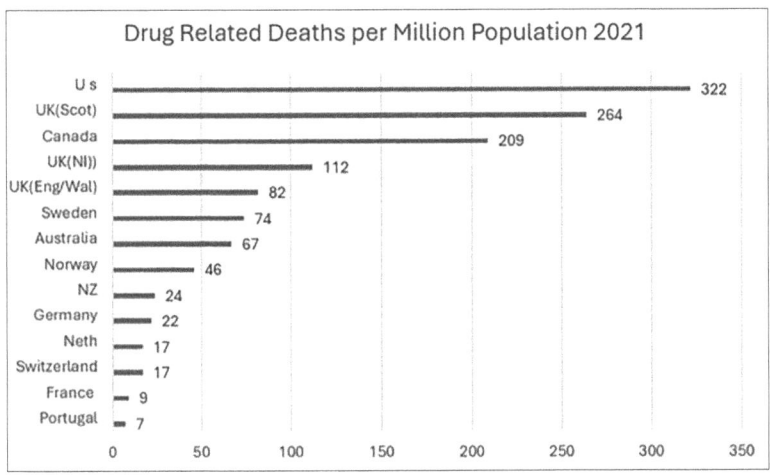

Figure 9-3 Drug Relate Deaths per Million Population Source: Commonwealth Fund.

Another reason for the reduced life expectancy in the United States compared to other developed countries is its relatively higher maternal death rate. As shown in Figure 9-4, there were 17.4 such deaths in the United State, more than double those in the next highest number of deaths—France at 8.7, and Canada at 8.6. Again, since women giving birth are of a relatively young age their deaths

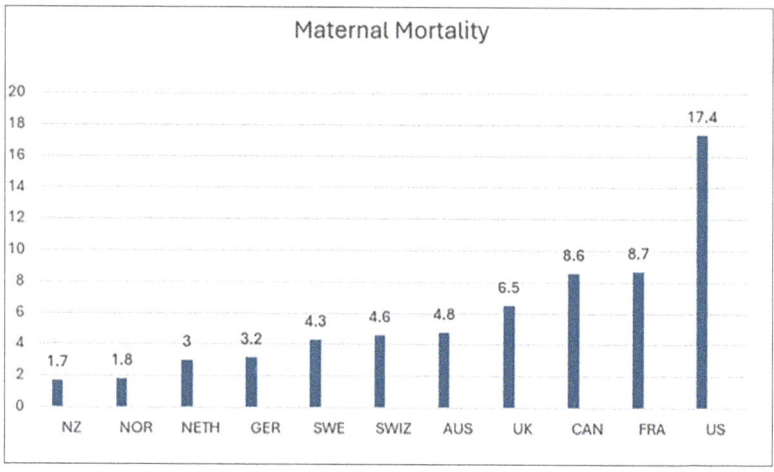

Figure 9-4. Maternal Mortality Ratios in Selected Developed Countries, 2018 or Latest Year. Source: Roosa Tikkanen et al. *Maternal Mortality and Maternal Care in the United States Compared to 10 Other Developed Countries*, The Commonwealth Fund, Nov. 2020 contribute disproportionately to the reduction in life expectance in the United States.

These factors—obesity, gun deaths, drug disorders, and maternal mortality—are only several of the characteristics in American society which contribute to shortened lives. There are others, such as the increased use of high-speed automobiles with distracted drivers, which contribute, but the salient point is that they are known, and subject to behavioral changes which could reverse this downward trend in American life expectancy.

B. Health Care

A study by The Commonwealth Fund in 2021 compared health care in eleven high income countries.[10] The study focused on Access to Care, Care Process, Administrative Efficiency, Equity, and Health Care Outcomes.

Regarding Access to Care, the emphasis was on affordability and timeliness, or who can afford to pay for it, and is it available when needed. A primary differentiator among nations is universal health care and most nations, except for the United States, have some version of care available to everyone. As a result, the United States ranked last among the eleven nations evaluated.

The area of Care Process, or how the care is provided, includes preventive, safe, and coordinated care, such as that between primary and specialized doctors. This is the one category in which the United States excels, ranking second among the nations evaluated.

The third category is Administrative Process, which includes areas such as getting insurance approval, billing for care, and other documentation related to getting and receiving care. As expected, the United States ranks eleventh among the study's nations, and is probably due to the complex relationship between government health care providers (Medicare, Medicaid, etc.) and the health care insurance industries.

Another category in The Commonwealth Fund study is Equity, specifically differences in income, but not racial or other socioeconomic differences, due to the difficulty of acquiring standardized data for these. However, the differences between higher- and lower-income groups regarding the quality of care are among the most diverse of the nations evaluated, with the United States again ranking last.

Finally, the area of Health Care Outcomes reflects the degree to which a nation is successful in achieving health outcomes such as life expectancy, infant and maternal mortality, and avoidable mortality. Unfortunately, the United States ranks poorly in all these outcomes. With regard to infant mortality, the United States ranks highest (worst) among the nations evaluated at 5.7 deaths per 1,000 live births. And U.S. life expectancy (at 23.1 years past the age of 60) is the lowest among the nations evaluated. Also, as already noted, U.S. maternal mortality rate of 17.4 deaths per 1,000 live births is more than twice the rate of the next highest mortality rate of 8.7 deaths per 1,000 live births in France.

In sum, the United States ranks last among the nations evaluated in all these measures except Care Process.

Of possibly even greater significance is the amount, expressed as a percentage of Gross Domestic Product, each of these nations spends on health care. For various reasons not covered in the study, the United States spends a much higher percentage of GDP (16.8 percent) on health care than the other high-income nations, which spend between 5 and 8 percent of GDP.[10]

Perhaps one of the most significant lessons learned from the study is the importance of universal health care. Especially in the areas of Access to Care and Equity, the fact that all citizens of the high-income nations with some form of universal health care score highest in these areas attests to its value. Conversely, the United States is the only nation among high income countries without universal health care, and this is reflected in its low scores in these areas.

Also, the study revealed the importance of primary care in delivering effective health care. The nations scoring highest in the study all emphasized the importance of ensuring the availability of excellent primary care to all communities regardless of income or racial differences.

The nations scoring highest in all areas of health care consistently demonstrated reductions in administrative burdens, which allowed these nations to invest more time and resources to actually providing high quality health care.

Finally, and perhaps a little unsurprising, is the value of social services in providing effective health care. Placing an emphasis on education, nutrition, and childcare improve the likelihood of a nation being successful in delivering effective health care for all its citizens.

III. Sustainable Development Impact

A. Health and Well-Being

So important is the existence of health to sustainable development that it is designated as United Nations Sustainable Development Goal 3 (Good Health and Well-Being) among its 17 Goals, and there are many reasons for this. Non-communicable diseases such as cancer and cardiovascular disease cause 63 percent of all deaths worldwide, and AIDs, tuberculosis, malaria, COVID-19, and other viral diseases add to the number of deaths. As a result, the absence of good health brought on by disease, both communicable and non-communicable, is one of the main reasons affecting sustainable development in Third World countries.

To achieve the intent of this goal, the UN has developed nine targets to actually focus attention by those seeking results in sustainable development by 2030. Among these is a reduction in global maternal deaths from 223 per 100,000 live births currently to less than 70.[11]

A second target seeks to eliminate preventable deaths among children under five years of age. This would reduce the deaths in newborns to 12 per 1,000 live births, and deaths to children under five years of age to 25 per 1,000 live births – again, by 2030.

Another target focuses on AIDS, tuberculosis, and malaria epidemics, tropical diseases, and other communicable diseases, seeking the elimination of these per 1,000 population by 2030.

Also, by 2030, a fourth target of Goal 3 is a one-third reduction in the percent mortality rate of those at age thirty who would die before age seventy from non-communicable diseases such as diabetes, cardiovascular disease, and cancer, and from mental health disability leading to suicide.

Currently, significant parts of the populations of both developed and undeveloped nations suffer from substance and alcohol abuse, which affects sustainable development. This is especially acute in the United States where there are over 322 drug-related deaths annually per one million population—the most of any developed nation—as noted previously. The intent of a fifth Goal 3 target is the prevention and treatment of substance abuse.

Each year there are over 1.35 million deaths on roadways caused by vehicles including cars, motorcycles, trucks, and busses, and more than half of these deaths are among cyclists, motorcyclists, and pedestrians.[12] When the UN's Sustainable Development Goals were developed, this problem was so acute that this sixth target – to half the number of such deaths – was set for 2020 rather than 2030. In December of 2021, this number was still 1.3 million, and the goal of this target was to reduce that number by half by 2030.

Especially from the standpoint of sustainable development is there a need for access to sexual and reproductive care, including family planning and education. Universal access to such care is thus the intent of the seventh target of UN Sustainable Development Goal 3.

The intent of the eighth target—Achieve Universal Health Coverage—requires some explanation. While much of the world does have universal coverage, except sub-Saharan Africa, many of these areas provide such coverage at a cost. The United States is one example where there is such coverage because it's often offered as a benefit of employment at large successful companies or provided as a social service such as Medicaid for those in need, or as Medicare for those over sixty-five, and those who don't fall into one of these categories can often be treated in emergency rooms or urgent care faculties as a charitable service.

In areas such as sub-Saharan Africa where there is no, or little, health care, and it is these areas of the world for which this target it intended. Especially for rampant infectious diseases, such as malaria, which are common in Africa, but virtually unheard of in the developed world, this target provides a possible path to sustainable development.

Finally, the ninth target – Reduce Illnesses and Deaths from Hazardous Chemicals and Pollution – addresses the most ubiquitous cause of death throughout the world. Even in supposedly the more highly developed nations such as the United States, there are areas near oil refineries in Houston or Long Beach – often populated by lower socioeconomic populations – which suffer disproportionately from harmful air quality. Again, in many areas of sub-Saharan Africa, people suffer from harmful indoor air quality from cooking with indoor stoves and fireplaces. For several reasons, air pollution and hazardous chemicals prevent sustainable development in many parts of the world.

In addition to the direct reference to Health and Well-Being of Goal 3, several of the other sustainable development goals affect health in related ways. Among these is Goal 1: No Poverty. The connection between poverty and poor health is seen in so many ways. In countries without universal health care, the ability to see a doctor or to be treated in a hospital is directly related to having the financial resources to pay, and those without such resources are unable to get regular checkups or delay the progression of disease. And those living in poorer neighborhoods (food deserts) often do not have access to healthy foods.

The second UN sustainable goal—Zero Hunger—also relates to health since good nutrition is necessary for human growth, especially among children. Even in those cases where hunger is satisfied, it's often with non-nutritious, processed or "junk" foods, which leads to obesity or otherwise poor health. In any case, hunger is a major impediment to sustainable development. And a more direct cause of poor health is that addressed by Goal 6—Clean water and Sanitation. Taken for granted in developed countries, the lack of clean water in so many parts of the world, especially in the already mentioned nations of sub-Saharan Africa, is often the cause of communicable diseases such as malaria, tuberculosis, and typhoid fever. In fact, children in areas of the world where there is little or no safe drinking water are twenty times more likely to die as a result of water-borne disease.

Goal 10 of the UN's Sustainable Development Goals is Reduced Inequality. Especially regarding unequal access to adequate health care in which those of lower socioeconomic position are unable to access health care, this goal seeks to make it (health care) available to all. Without it, large segments of the population are unable to contribute to the sustainable development of the nation.

Finally, Goal 14: Life Below water, can also have a direct health impact on sustainable development. This is because without clean oceans, rivers, and lakes, much of the world's population is deprived of an important source of protein in seafood. In the worst cases of industrial pollution, contaminated bodies of water not only deprive many people of a source of protein, but also lead to the spread of infectious disease.

B. Health Care

According to the Sustainable Development Solutions Network of the United Nations, health (and, by inference, health care) is central to sustainable development. As such, "societies commit to progress across four dimensions: economic development including the eradication of extreme poverty, social inclusion, environmental sustainability, and good governance."

With regard to the first of these—economic development—the central question must be, "Who pays for the health care provided?" This is especially true since those most frequently using heath care in the twentieth century were retirees sixty to sixty-five years of age, whereas those in the twenty-first century were at least eighty. In other words, people are living longer and depending on the type of health care system in a given country, financial contributions from the labor class will be insufficient to provide the required degree of health care. The solution to this dilemma would likely be an increase in taxes to satisfy this shortfall.

Again, depending on the type of health care system in a given nation, increased taxation would have different impacts on different socioeconomic classes. In the United States, where health care is largely financed by a combination of contributions from employers and labor, more affluent members of society can absorb the increased costs, whereas those less affluent have a more difficult time getting health care, often doing without. Thus, the issue of social inclusion is one which should be addressed when considering the sustainability of health care. This is especially true when it is considered that health care is a human right, and not something which depends on those able to afford it. There are 85 million Americans today who are either uninsured or underinsured, and 60,000 people die each year because they couldn't see a doctor.[16]

Another sustainability issue in health care is that having to do with the environment. Among several environmental impacts is that having to do with climate change, specifically, the emission of greenhouse gases stemming from health care operations including hospital emissions, transportation, and medical procedures. According to one estimate in 2019, health care is responsible for 4.4 per cent of the total greenhouse gas emissions worldwide.[17] And in the United States alone, health care contributes 7.9 to 9.8 percent of the total emissions.[17] In addition to health care's effect on climate change, there are other environmental sustainability effects as well. These include the toxic effects of medical waste and the failure to recycle used medical equipment, surgical supplies, and paper. This failure contributes to overused landfills and ultimately disposal in the marine environment.

Finally, another area of sustainable development related to health care is good governance. The way in which a nation structures its health care system is directly related to decisions made, and actions taken by, its government. As noted earlier, the choice of a given heath care system as one of the four most common types (Beveridge, Bismarck, National Health Insurance, or Uninsured) is largely a function of who provides health care, and who pays for it. Unless the one receiving health care pays for it himself (uninsured) the cost of care is some combination of employer or the government through taxes. This choice is for the most part driven by government policy, which, in turn, is decided by people in a democratic society, or solely by the government in a more autocratic society. In any case, the availability of health care is primarily a function of government.

For true sustainability in health care to exist then, these four elements should exist simultaneously, that is, viable economics, social inclusion (health care is a human right), environmental sustainability, and good governance. Insofar as any of these is lacking, the health care system is not optimum from the standpoint of sustainable development.

IV. Leadership Opportunities in Addressing Health and Well-Being and Health Care

A. Government

The opportunities for leadership in health care depend, to a great extent, on the type of health care system in a given country, one in which there is universal coverage, as defined earlier, or one in which its citizens have no coverage, or uninsured coverage.

The first of these, universal coverage, according to one of the three models described earlier, is the predominant one in most of the high-income countries of the world. While there are many different types, depending on who provides and delivers the health care, they are all pretty much distinguished by the availability at low or no cost to everyone needing it. One example is the National Health Service (NHS) of Great Britain. While there are opportunities to obtain private health insurance and care, for which about 13 percent of the population subscribes, the vast majority of British citizens access health care through the NHS. But the leadership role played by the NHS, and similar governments providing universal coverage, is one of guidance and regulation to optimize care. For the NHS, an example of this is the recent emphasis on improved health care provided by the Department of Health and Social Care which focused on, among other things

- clear leadership and management standards for NHS managers with a standardized appraisal system

- greater incentives for top talent to move into leadership roles in areas facing the greatest challenges, to help combat disparities across the country[18]

In the case of uninsured coverage, best typified among high-income nations by the United States, the opportunities for leadership in government exist in at least two ways. One, congressional leaders have often introduced legislation to establish some type of single payer health care plan which would effectively provide universal coverage. One such plan is the frequently mentioned "Medicare for All" patterned after the popular and successful Medicare program which currently provides health care to those sixty-five and above. Unfortunately, this and other universal coverage programs have not had any success in being implemented, due primarily to political differences.

The other avenue for leadership by government in health care is in oversight and the establishment of standards and best practices by those not providing universal coverage. In the United States this role is provided by the various regulatory agencies, such as the Department of Health & Human Services (HHS), the Federal Drug Administration (FDA), and the Centers for Medicare and Medicaid (CMS). And it is up to the leaders of these agencies to exercise their responsibilities to ensure safe and effective health care to all citizens regardless of their position in society or ability to pay.[19]

B. Businesses and Corporations

According to a report by the U.S. Surgeon General, business has a significant role to play in promoting effective health care.[20] In *Community Health and Economic Prosperity: Engaging Businesses as Stewards and Stakeholders*, Vice Admiral Dr. Jerome Adams describes the ways in which businesses can more effectively do this. Specifically, the report covers four ways in which they can promote better health care: 1) they can listen to their stakeholders including suppliers and communities on issues of health care; 2) they should create a culture of their business's combined effect on health and the economy; 3) they should form partnerships with other businesses to promote effective health care; and 4), they should collect data to measure the impact of these efforts at improving health care.

As an example of how this can be done, Dr. Doug Jutte, a primary care physician and one of the authors of the report, notes that hospitals charge $800 billion a year for amputating feet as a result of Type 2 diabetes. A better use of resources, he says, is taking measures to avoid the onset of diabetes, such as behavioral counseling and education to reduce the incidence of Type 2 diabetes, and, hence, the need for eventual amputation. Such a restructuring of priorities would require leadership on the part of both businesses and the medical profession.

C. Individual

The opportunities to exercise leadership in good health – especially personal leadership – from physical exercise are obvious, in as much as each of us can encourage others to exercise. And nearly as important is the value of good nutrition, or a healthy diet, has also been noted in an earlier chapter, and everyone can influence others in this. What has not as often been discussed is the value of good health in social relationships. A study in the Proceedings of the National Academy of Sciences has shown that social relationships can be as important to good health as either exercise or nutrition.[21] Simply maintaining an extensive social network has proven to benefit good health in even heretofore unsuspected physical manifestations such as a reduction in inflammation. Furthermore, social interaction has been shown to be of benefit at all stages of life. And it's not necessarily the quality of relationships always but rather the extent of such relationships, or the number of such relationships one has.

This aspect of good health is especially pertinent to the subject of leadership in advancing sustainable development. By their very nature social relationships imply the opportunities for leadership. Enjoying cycling or hiking with others, or even convincing them to participate, is an element of leadership. And in this sense, social relationships are, in fact, ways to promote good health in others as well as in oneself.

V. Examples of Leadership in Advancing Health and Heath Care

A. Government

The Affordable Care Act, also known as the Patient Protection and Affordable Care Act, or simply as Obamacare, was passed by Congress in 2010, and is an excellent example of government leadership in advancing sustainable development. Good health and effective health care is so important to sustainability that it is included as one of the United Nations 13 Goals in Sustainable Development to be achieved by 2030. And it is particularly applicable to leadership given the opposition to its passage in Congress by some fearing their loss of influence, and since then given the many challenges it faced by the same opposition. But fortunately, strong leadership in the White House, Supreme Court and Congress have met these challenges to where the ACA is now the law of the land.

At its most basic the ACA provides increased access to insurance for those not having it, expanded consumer protection from the companies providing it, preventive care which was not afforded under many insurance plans, and improved health quality at lower costs.[22] Prior to the ACA many health insurance plans previously would not cover certain preexisting illnesses, but the ACA covers these. Though the penalty for not enrolling in an approved health insurance plan has been contested by Congress and many state legislatures, these objections have been overruled by many federal courts as well as the United States Supreme Court. The victories in these decisions are testimony to the leadership shown by these government bodies.

By almost any measure the ACA has been a resounding success.[23] After the first ten years of its existence there are 20 million people now ensured due to the ACA, and 12 million more are now covered under Medicaid. The ACA also addressed some of the glaring disparities inherent before ACA. In expansion states, the difference in coverage between white and black adults was reduced by more than half, and the difference in coverage between white and Hispanic adults was reduced by almost half. Moreover, because of ACA, increased access to health care for those receiving Medicaid saw improved health outcomes to the extent of 19,000 lives being saved.

Finally, public perception of the success of the ACA is evident from poll results. Public approval of the ACA went from

34 percent in 2011 to 53 percent in 2020. Clearly, government leadership in improving both the universal access and improved effectiveness of health care was validated in the ten years after its passage in the United States.

B. Businesses and Corporations—The Walt Disney Company[24]

An excellent example of what private corporations can do to advance the quality of health and health care for both employees and communities is The Walt Disney Company. It has done this by shifting the emphasis of providing health care to its 77,000 employees at Walt Disney World in Orlando, Florida, from a traditional "fee for service" model to one in which fees are based on the quality of care provided. In the former approach fees are based on the volume of services provided rather than the quality of services as reflected in lower rates of infection, hospital readmittance, and surgery complications. It does this by reducing overall costs which result from a healthier workforce through its emphasis on quality of care. And it's able to do this by negotiating with hospitals and insurance providers for payments more reflective of this approach.

As a result of this approach, and in recognition of its effort to implement value-based health care for its employees, the nonprofit Business Group on Health presented The Walt Disney Company with The Helen Darling Award for Excellence in Health Care Value and Innovation. Disney began this effort in 2018 in cooperation with Orlando Health and Florida Hospital, and continues providing leadership in health and health care as part of its sustainable development.

C. Individual– Ella Watson-Stryker

Ella Watson-Stryker is one of seven named as Time Magazine's 2014 Persons of the Year for their work inconfronting the Ebola Virus in Guinea, Sierra Leone and Liberia. Not herself a Medical Doctor, she was the Humanitarian Affairs Officer in Doctors Without Borders. Along with the six others included in the recognition, it reads "For their tireless acts of courage and mercy, for buying the world time to strengthen its defenses, for the risks they took and the lives they saved, they faced the Ebola Virus". Interestingly, her degree from Rutgers University in geography and religion demonstrated what can be done without being a Medical Doctor, but willing to subject oneself to the danger of contagion in providing information to those threatened by the disease. In this role she has exemplified significant leadership in halting the spread of the Ebola Virus.

References

1. Adam Felman, *What is good health?* MedicalNewsToday, April 19, 2020.
2. *Benefits of Physical Activity*, National Center for Chronic Disease Prevention and Health Promotion, June 16, 2022.
3. Pedro F. Saint-Maurice, PhD, Barry I. Grauber, PhD, Richard P. Troiano, PhD, et.al., *Estimated Number of Deaths Prevented Through Increased Physical Activity Among US Adults*, JAMA Network, Jan. 24, 2022.
4. Felman, *What is good health?*
5. *Top Ten Reasons Why Mental Health Is So Important*, planstreetinc.com, Nov. 24, 2021.
6. *Quality of care*, World Health Organization.

7. Alex Evans, *4 Types of Healthcare System Designs—and the Pros and Cons of Each*, GoodRxHealth, Nov. 9, 2022.
8. John Gramlich, *Gun deaths among U.S. children and teens rose 50% in two years*, Pew Research Center, April 6, 2023.
9. Jesse C. Baumgartner, Evan D. Gumas, Munira , Gunja, *Too Many Lives Lost: Comparing Overdose Mortality Rates and Policy Solutions Across High-Income Countries*, Commonwealth Fund, May 19, 2022.
10. Eric C. Schneider, et al, *Mirror, Mirror, 2021, Reflecting Poorly: Reflecting Poorly Health in the U.S. Compared to Oher High Income Countries*, The Commonwealth Fund, August 4, 2021.
11. Roni Cary Rabin, *Global Declines in Maternal Mortality Have Stalled*, NY Times, Feb. 22, 2023.
12. *Road Traffic Injuries and Deaths—A Global Problem*, Centers for Disease Control and Prevention, January 10, 2023.
13. *Global Public Health: 2022's Sustainable Development Goals Report*, Keck School of Medicine of USC, March 21, 2023.
14. Lauren Barredo et al, *Health in the Framework of Sustainable Development*, Health in the Framework of Sustainable Development, 18 February 2014.
15. Lycourgos Liaropoulos and llias Goranitis, *Health care financing and the sustainability of health systems*, International Journal for Equity in Health, September 15, 2915.
16. Bernie Sanders, *It's time to guarantee healthcare to all Americans as a human right*, The Guardian, May 18, 2023.
17. Hensher, *Health Care Sustainability Metric: Building a Safer, Low-Carbon Health System.*
18. *Biggest shake-up in health and social care leadership in a generation to improve patient care*, Department of Health and Social Care, June 8, 2022.
19. Dr. Liji Thomas, MD, *What is the Role of Regulatory Bodies in Healthcare?* News-Medical, December 7, 2021.
20. Jeff Lagasse, *Business has a role to play in increasing healthcare quality and access, says Surgeon General report*, HealthCareIT-News, Jan. 19, 2021.

21. Elahe Izadi, *Your relationships are just as important to your health as diet and exercise*, Washington Post, January 5, 2016.
22. Will Kenton, *Affordable Care Act (ACA): What It Is, Key Features, and Updates*, Investopedia, Sept 22, 2023.
23. Sarah Somers, *The Affordable Care Act: Reflections on 10 Years*, The Network for Public Health Law, May 6, 2021.
24. Deanna Cuadra, *Why Disney shifted to a value-based care model for its 77,000 Florida employees*, ebn, February 22, 2023
25. David von Drehe, Aryn Baker, *The Ebola Fighters, The Ones Who Answered The Call*, Time Magazine, Dec 10, 2014

10

Summary and Conclusions

Sustainable development is usually illustrated by the presence of three distinguishing characteristics, often called The Triple Bottom Line: 1) the Environment; 2) Economics; and 3) Social Equity. It is so designated due to its relationship to financial performance. Leadership plays a critical role in fulfilling all these areas of sustainable development. With regard to social equity, which is simply how one person in society treats another person, this is evident in at least three levels.

In communities, members of a given group often treat others with varying degrees of respect (or disrespect) because of certain distinguishing characteristics, such as socioeconomic status, race, religion, or some other perceived difference. This may lead to unequal availability of housing, unfair treatment in education, or other discriminatory attitudes and behaviors.

At the national level certain groups receive better or worse treatment, again, because of race, religion, economic positions, or other characteristics. The caste system in India is one example which comes to mind. While there have been tremendous improvements in race relations in the United States, there are still some vestiges of unequal treatment of people of color in health care, housing opportunities, and the availability of credit for some major purchases.

Another level in which social equity (or lack thereof) is evident is that among individuals. Consider the difference in treatment of people of color by some members of law enforcement or the perceived differences in the treatment people of color accorded by teachers, school administrators, or others in positions of authority.

It's important to keep in mind the relationship between social equity and the other two elements of The Triple Bottom Line: the environment and economics. It's no secret that the worst effects of climate change are often felt by those least able to avoid them. It's a fact that neighboring populations of people of color are often located around polluting refineries or other industries. Similarly, the disparity in lower-income employment and lower overall wealth between people of color and whites is strikingly obvious, and there are glaring disparities in other areas such as home ownership and financial security.

There is a need for leadership in addressing these inequalities. Specifically, there is a need to redirect the behavior of those charged with protecting the environment, managing the economic performance of all nations, and protecting the human rights of those who need protection. These leadership skills are to be found among those individuals involved in public administration, those involved in managing businesses and industries, and perhaps most importantly, those in the military, for in no other endeavor are leadership skills in managing people as highly valued as among those men and women charged with leading others in the defense of their country. In other words, there is a need for leadership in achieving sustainable development goals throughout all elements of society.

It's helpful to consider the definition of leadership attributed to former President Dwight Eisenhower. Though probably said with military performance in mind, it is especially apropos to achieving sustainable development.

> *Leadership is the art of getting someone else to do something you want done because he wants to do it.*

This definition conveys the necessity of leading others to accomplish a goal by identifying and emphasizing those aspects of a goal—in this case sustainable development—which appeal most to those being led such that they pursue them of their own volition (they actually *want* to pursue them). The leadership traits which are conducive to this include communication, vision, presence, attitude, responsibility, respect, and empathy.

A review of the most effective leaders in history shows why this might be true. Among these leaders are Abraham Lincoln, Nelson Mandela, Frederick Douglas, FDR, Harriet Tubman, Ruth Bader Ginsburg, Dietrich Bonhoeffer, Martin Luther King, Jr., Malala Yousafzai, and Pope Francis. These leaders exemplify one or more of these leadership traits to varying degrees.

Possibly the best way to demonstrate the value of leadership in advancing the elements of sustainable development is to show its specific impact on several social equity issues particularly in need of it.

The first of these is one of the most detrimental and challenging social issues affecting society both worldwide and in the United States—*racism*. According to Race Forward there are four levels of racism: 1) internalized, 2) interpersonal, 3) institutional, and 4) structural. The first of these—internalized—is how one feels personally about race. Interpersonal racism is that which occurs when a person lets his personal feelings about race affect his or her behavior toward others. And institutional racism is that which occurs *within* institutions such as education, finance, or law enforcement. But structural racism is that which occurs because of a combinations of these three types of racism built into society and its institutions.

Few issues in sustainable development—particularly in the United States—are as significant as racism. Consider the unequal treatment of draftees during the Vietnam War, or the higher percentages of unemployment among black Americans, or the higher percentages of black Americans stricken with COVID during the 2020–2023 pandemic. All these inequities have affected the sustainable development of not only black Americans, but the country in general.

There continue to be many opportunities for leadership in addressing the inequities of racism in our society. Some examples of those who have distinguished themselves as leaders in this effort include former President Lyndon Johnson, possibly the individual most responsible for the Civil Rights Act of 1965. Others include baseball official Branch Rickey, and civil rights activist Rosa Parks, best known for her refusal to give up her seat on a bus in Montgomery in 1955.

Today, the most pervasive and growing issue of social equity, especially in large cities, is homelessness. Officially defined as *not having a home or permanent place of residence*, this definition almost trivializes one of the most serious problems in American society. While there are several different ways to estimate the number of homeless in the United States and worldwide, all show an increase in the most recent decades. In the United States the number of homeless in the 2010 census was 49 percent higher than in the 2000 census. And the number of homeless in some other countries per 100,000 population is even higher than in the United States with that in France at 216 versus 177 in the United States.

The impact of homelessness on sustainable development is significant, both to the individual experiencing it, and to society in general. Not having a place to call home is not only a blow to one's dignity, but a hindrance to achieving the security which so many of us take for granted. With regard to society, there are health and environmental impacts which result from having so many unhoused people living in unsafe and unsanitary conditions. Aside from the affected physical environment resulting from the homeless population's attempting to scrape by in tents or otherwise seeking shelter from the elements, there is the real danger of communicable diseases spreading from common living environments.

Despite the persistent challenge of addressing the growing problem of homelessness, there are numerous opportunities being pursued by government, businesses, and individuals to find solutions. Perhaps one of the most effective approaches is that taken by Father Joe Carroll in San Diego. Before passing away in 2021, Father Joe established a system to provide general care and shelter to scores of homeless citizens in his adopted city of San Diego.

Underlying the plight of many in lower socioeconomic classes is food and nutrition insecurity. Included in this are four conditions, any one of which could preclude food security. The first of these is availability, which means simply that enough food is being produced. For various reasons, though, such as climate change, enough food cannot be had by those who need it. Even if there is available food, people in need of it may not have access to it because of difficult transportation, supply chain disruption, or political instability. Even if there is available food, and those who need it have access to it, food utilization may be such that preparation and content of the food is not adequate to provide the required nutrients. Finally, all these characteristics have to be satisfied on an ongoing basis to provide a degree of stability in providing nutrition security.

Summary and Conclusions

The degree of food insecurity varies significantly throughout the world. For various reasons, it is much more pronounced in sub-Saharan Africa, the Middle East, and parts of Latin America. Even in the United States, large parts of the population are food insecure, especially in the food deserts common in lower socioeconomic parts of inner cities and outside the cities.

Almost all the UN Sustainability Goals relate in some way to food insecurity, but Goal 2—End Hunger—addresses it specifically. Sustainable development is inconceivable whenever populations—especially children—do not have enough nutritious food for healthy development.

There are numerous opportunities for governments, business organizations, and individuals to address food insecurity throughout the world. Especially worthy of mention is World Central Kitchen—an international nonprofit founded by Jose Andres in 2010 to help those afflicted by natural disasters to secure much needed food.

Another societal problem crying out for leadership at all levels is poverty and income inequality. Fundamentally, poverty is not having the basic necessities of life, and it affects significant parts of the population in many parts of the world, especially in sub-Saharan Africa and the Middle East. But the related issue of income inequality is potentially more far reaching in the number of lives affected. The degree of income inequality is shown graphically by the Lorenz Curve, which plots the total cumulative wealth of a nation (the y-axis) versus the percent of the total population (the x-axis). Points above the curve could show a greater degree of income for a segment of the population, and points below it could show a lower degree of income for that segment of the population.

As noted, certain parts of the world exhibit drastic poverty, but income inequality is prevalent even in developed nations and usually defines the differences between upper and lower socioeconomic classes. The effects of poverty on sustainable development are a function of these differences. In the cases of extreme poverty, much of the population must resort to environmental degradation, such as deforestation, simply to provide enough food for families. But even in more developed nations, much of the populations is unable to contribute to sustainable development due to its preoccupation with simply achieving the basic necessities of life.

There are opportunities for leadership at all levels. In government there is a special need for leadership among those willing to espouse issues which clearly affect income inequality, and business organizations can lead in ensuring fair compensation for their workers and not just wealthy shareholders. Individuals too, have a role to play, if only in advocating for equity in compensating all members of society.

Among the best-known examples of leadership in government has to have been that shown by President Franklin Delano Roosevelt in his New Deal programs confronting the Great Depression. Similarly, President Lyndon Johnson had the goal of improved treatment of all Americans in his Great Society programs.

Almost defining the overriding issue of social equity are the related issues of social and environmental justice. Generally, social justice pertains to the fair distribution of the benefits of economic growth to everyone, regardless of their origin or place in society. More specifically, environmental justice addresses the equal treatment of everyone regarding the laws, policies, and regulations pertaining to the environment.

Regarding social justice, there are five characteristics of the availability of societal benefits. The first of these is access, meaning all members of society can seek and obtain these benefits. Also, this access is predicated on equity, or fairness, to all in their desire to achieve them. Specifically, this access is available to all without consideration of race, gender or other characteristics, and participation is guaranteed for all. Finally, in all cases of social interaction and achieving these benefits, Human Rights is of the greatest concern.

Unfortunately, certain common assumptions drive both social and environmental injustice. The first of these is that humans are exploitable, meaning that their treatment is bound by nothing other than the fact that they are useful. Similarly, many people assume that the environment is exploitable, and as with respect to human beings, their only concern is what benefit can be achieved through its use, regardless of the harm done to it. In the Third World many people have no recourse except to abide by this type of treatment of themselves and the environment with predictable harm to both.

The sustainability impact of social and environmental injustice goes directly to the second and third elements of The Triple Bottom Line, economics and social equity respectively. The impact of economics is seen every day throughout the world and in the United States. Clearly, the conditions under which much of the world's poor live are an affront to common decency and the failure of society to provide the most basic necessities of life in the form of shelter, food, and water. Even in the United States, the fact that people of color and lower socioeconomic status are often forced to live in the most environmentally toxic locations is only one example of environmental injustice.

The UN's Sustainability Goals specifically address social and environmental justice in Goals Goal 1, 10, and 16—No Poverty, Reduced Inequalities, and Peace, Justice, and Strong Institutions. As might be expected, the leadership opportunities in these areas are especially evident in government, but also in business organizations and the individual. As already mentioned, FDR's New Deal is possibly the best example of what government can do to advance social and environmental justice. But businesses can also play a prominent role, as Ben & Jerry's—the iconic quality ice cream company—has shown time and again with its support of social and environmental issues.

One of the most pressing social issues today—both worldwide and in the U.S.—is that having to do with immigration, refugees, and asylum seekers. Regarding the extent of each of these throughout the world, immigrants comprise by far the greatest number, totaling 280.6 million. While the number is far smaller for refugees—27.1 million—the circumstances of refugees, such as the forces driving them out of their countries and their physical transport, are far more tragic. Consider the numbers crowded into boats trying to make the journey across the Mediterranean to reach Greece or Italy. While the number of asylum seekers is even smaller at 4.9 million, their circumstances are similarly tragic. Consider the thousands of asylum seekers escaping conditions in Central Americas, traveling thousands of miles north, and crossing the Rio Grande to attempt entry into the United States under the most hazardous conditions. The differences of these people leaving their countries aside, their effects on sustainable development are similar.

As noted earlier, significant environmental impacts follow from many of these displaced persons doing whatever is necessary to survive, such as clearing forests for agriculture and burning waste to prepare food. Again, the UN Sustainability Goals specifically address these humanitarian issues: Hunger, Quality Education, Clean Water and Sanitation—Goals 1, 4, and 6 respectively.

Regarding leadership opportunities, most of these are at the government level, as the movement of large groups of people is often instigated by government policies or failure thereof. But businesses and corporations have a role to play in either welcoming or deterring those who have left their original countries for better lives. Within these businesses and especially Non-Governmental Organizations, there are individuals who can exercise leadership.

One of the best examples of leadership at the governmental level, at least in the United States, is the DACA (Deferred Action for Childhood Arrivals) program. At the risk of political blowback, the Obama administration developed this program, which has withstood challenges to its implementation which continue to this day.

Among businesses and corporations, there are also examples of leadership which not only improve the welfare of these displaced persons but enhance the economic performance of these companies. Among these companies are IKEA and Adidas, which have shown not only a humanitarian priority, but also that this strategy is financially profitable as well.

At the individual level, one particular name stands out in history for his contribution to improving the lives of refugees. Varian Fry was a thirty-two-year-old American journalist the Emergency Rescue Committee sent to France in 1940 to aid refugees in that country who were fleeing the Germans. Operating out of a hotel, he helped 1,500 refugees escape the Nazis and provided assistance to another 2,400 living in occupied France. So successful was he in these efforts that the Germans expelled him from the country.

Possibly the most striking example of leadership improving the lives and welfare of others is in the areas of *Health and Health Care*. This is probably because the existence of good health—both physical and mental—depends on the decisions and acts of others in providing it. This is especially true in governments which determine the type and extent of health care provided.

According to the WHO "Health is a state of complete physical, mental, and social well-being and not merely the absence of disease or infirmity." The WHO further expands this definition by "emphasizing social and personal resources, as well as physical capacities," which call out the need for leadership. The inclusion of good mental health, along with good physical health, underlines the need for leadership given its critical role in relating to others.

Especially pertinent to good health—both physical and mental—is the way health care is provided in society. From a leadership standpoint, the degree of success in providing good health care is often determined by the choice of one of the four most common health care models: Beveridge, Bismarck, National health insurance, or Uninsured.

In assessing the success of health and health care throughout the world it is helpful to compare the United States with other developed countries. Regarding the degree of health, life expectancy serves as one metric, with that in the U.S. at 76.1 years and 82.4 years for other developed countries. Regarding health care, the U.S. again fares poorly, coming in last among developed countries in the weighted average of various health care metrics. Among the presumed reasons for the poor performance of the U.S. in these metrics are the exceptional degree of gun deaths, drug addictions, and the absence of universal health care.

With regard to the sustainability impact of health, the UN Sustainability Goal 3—Good Health and Well-Being—directly addresses it (health) specifically. After all, what can ensure the sustainable development of society more directly than the good health of its citizens? Indirectly, the importance of good health is addressed also in Goals 1, 2, and 6 (NO Poverty, Zero Hunger, and Clean Water and Sanitation, respectively).

Health care may have an even more important relation to sustainable development. Consider the role of economics in ensuring the availability and delivery of good health care. Or, put another way, how important is social inclusion in ensuring the availability of health care to all of a country's population regardless of race or socioeconomic position? Or how important is concern for the environment when considering the second and third order effects of health care, such as the energy required for its delivery, or the impact of disposing of the materials used in providing health care services. Finally, how can health care be delivered to a country's citizens except through the decisions of governments to ensure its delivery—indicative of the role government plays in sustainable development?

There are many leadership opportunities in ensuring good health and, by implication, effective health care in all countries. Perhaps governments have the greatest opportunity to ensure the good health and health care of their citizens by implementing one of the health care models mentioned earlier. One glaring example in the United States is the Affordable Care Act, also known as Obama Care, which provided a degree of health care not previously available to many people.

Businesses and corporations also have a role in advancing good health and health care, as demonstrated by The Walt Disney Corporation in Orlando, Florida.

As with many of the leadership opportunities in issues of social equity being available to individuals, these exist also in health and health care. One notable example is Ella Watson-Stryker, one of seven individuals recognized by Time Magazine as Persons of the Year in 2014 for their tireless work in saving lives from the Ebola Virus. While not a Medical Doctor, she used her education in religion and geography to show leadership in helping those potentially afflicted by the disease.

www.ingramcontent.com/pod-product-compliance
Lightning Source LLC
LaVergne TN
LVHW050620040125
800479LV00012B/156